Home town:

Philadelphia, PA

What inspired him to go into acting:

saw Yul Brynner in *The King and I* at
age seven

How he was discovered:

his manager spotted him walking his
dog and signed him on

First big break:

acting as Kelly Bundy's biker boyfriend
on *Married . . . with Children*

Hobbies:

Golf, bowling, skiing, basketball,
tennis—almost all sports

DAVID BOREANAZ

CHRIS NICKSON

St. Martin's Paperbacks

DAVID BOREANAZ

Copyright © 1999 by Chris Nickson.

Cover photograph by Nathaniel Welch/Outline.

All rights reserved. No part of this book may be used or reproduced
in any manner whatsoever without written permission except in the
case of brief quotations embodied in critical articles or reviews. For
information address St. Martin's Press, 175 Fifth Avenue, New York,
N.Y. 10010.

ISBN: 0-312-97361-6

Printed in the United States of America

St. Martin's Paperbacks edition / September 1999

10 9 8 7 6 5 4 3 2 1

ACKNOWLEDGMENTS

As always, it would be impossible to begin a book without offering my deepest thanks to my agent, Madeleine Morel. In the time we've worked together she's helped me in many ways, and I truly appreciate every one of them. For me, she's quite honestly the best in the business.

It's a pleasure to work once again with John Rounds. Some four and a half years have elapsed since we did our first book together, and in that time he's become not only an editor, but also a friend, and it was his enthusiasm for this project that really gave it wings. Thank you.

There are four other people who need to be thanked every time I sit down to write. My wife, Linda, and my son, Graham. They keep me grounded and centered, and give me a reason to spend time away from the computer. Then Ray and Betty Nickson, my parents. They were the ones who encouraged me to write, and then kept pestering me when I didn't. Without their help, I probably wouldn't be sitting here to do this. I love you all.

For supplying materials, always superbly quick and thorough, my undying gratitude to Stephanie Ogle of Cinema Books in Seattle, one of my most treasured resources.

Friends, too, play their part: Jonathon and Judy Savill (as well as Jamie and Toby), Kevan Roberts, Christian Kent, John Taylor, Mike Murtagh, Fred and

Kath Davies, the members of the Leeds United Internet list (for helping my mornings be sane), Kevin Odell, Mitch Myers, Paul Clark and Cathy Sorbo, as well as a host of others who help make sure I don't vanish into a mist of words.

The following provided research material for the writing of this book: *Buffy the Vampire Slayer: The Watcher's Guide*, by Christopher Golden and Nancy Holder (Pocket Books); *The Girl's Got Bite*, by Kathleen Tracy (Renaissance Books); *Buffy X-Posed*, by Ted Edwards (Prima Books); "Horror Angel," by Mitch Persons, *Cinefantastique*, March 1999. "Star Struck Slayer," by Jenny Cooney Carrillo, *Dreamwatch*, March 1999; "Last Call," by Matt Springer, *Buffy the Vampire Slayer* magazine, Summer 1999; "Angel Earns his Wings," *Cinescape*, January/February 1999; *Vibe* Online Chat; "David Boreanaz—Actor," *People*, May 10, 1999; "David Boreanaz," by Ellen Scordato, *Best of the Boys*; "Give David A Cheesesteak," by Ellen Gray, *Philadelphia Daily News*, August 8, 1998; "Touched By Hell's Angel," by Kristen Baldwin, *Entertainment Weekly*, May 22, 1998; "TV Gal Talks To An Angel," by AmyTVGal, *AOL*; "City of Angel," by Dan Snierson, *Entertainment Weekly*, May 21, 1999; "Spinoff for *Buffy* Boyfriend," *USA Today*, June 26, 1998; "David Boreanaz," by Dorrie Crockett, *People Online*; "David Boreanaz," by Allan Johnson, *Chicago Tribune*; "So Far So Good," *Spectrum*, November 1998; "Buffy Babes: Juliet Landau," by Mitch Persons, *Femme Fatale*, October 1998; "The Scooby Gang," by Jean Cummings, *Xpose*, March 1999. "Vampires Beware," by Judy Sloane and Mark Wyman, *TV Zone*, October 1998.

DAVID BOREANAZ

INTRODUCTION

There are angels dark and light, and angels who are some of both, who walk both in the dark and in the light. Angels, of course, are forever, eternal. From earthly origins they've moved on to heaven. The devil was an angel until his rebellion against God, when he was cast out to hell. His followers accompanied him, giving up their angelic status for a different eternity. They are, if you will, the dark angels, the flipside of the coin.

Can an angel be a vampire? More to the point, can a vampire be an angel? Anyone who watches *Buffy the Vampire Slayer* knows the answers to those questions. If you're Angel, you can be both. You can be a vampire with a conscience, equally cursed and blessed, balancing love and hate, compassion and anger in one body that won't—that can't—die. His is a life that's carried him across the centuries and across the continents, a life that's a permanent limbo, a constant state of purgatory.

Angel is, naturally, a fiction. A remarkable one, but a fiction nonetheless. He's the creation of Joss Whedon, the man behind both *Buffy the Vampire Slayer*, the 1992 movie that took a lighthearted look at both vampires and high school, and the series on WB, which views everything through a much darker lens.

Angel has been Buffy's lover, and remains her great love but he's much more. In many ways, he's a part of her that she keeps hidden, even from herself.

Like God and the devil, Buffy and Angel are two sides of the same coin, the same person. It's something that they recognize in each other, but feel no need to say; they understand, and so do we.

Could there be an Angel walking among us? Possibly, but if so, he remains well hidden. There's no place like Sunnydale—at least, not the Sunnydale that's also Hellmouth. Sunnydale is Everytown, U.S.A. on the surface, but all the destruction caused by being the Hellmouth could never go unnoticed by the media. Maybe there really are vampires and slayers, maybe there truly is a world we sense a little but never quite manage to see. We seem to think so—hence our obsession with it. But we'll never know for sure.

One thing we can be certain of is the fact that David Boreanaz plays Angel, first on *Buffy* and now on *Angel*, his own series that takes him away from the suburban heaven (and hell) of Sunnydale to a real hell—Los Angeles. It's a mark not just of his looks, or his acting, but the power of his character—that interior battle between good and evil—that he's been spun off that way.

David's success has come almost accidentally, elevating him from just another struggling actor to one with his own series, the thing everyone in television aspires to. It's as if some force outside himself was guiding him to this role, which seems to fit him as well as any expensive glove. He was discovered for Angel in a way that was so perfectly Hollywood it just had to be true—if anyone had written it, it would have seemed like parody. Walking his dog, Bertha Blue, he was seen from a window by a manager who hurriedly signed him, then called the show's casting director, Marcia Schulman, who'd searched in vain for her Angel. An audition was arranged. The moment David walked into Schulman's office, she made a note on the casting sheet—"He's the guy." The tale of a young Lana Turner being spotted at the counter in Schwab's drugstore and groomed into a star is no more apocryphal.

You could say David was born to play Angel. The brooding look, the flashes of pain that cross his face, seem to come perfectly naturally. He can melt into the shadows, be there in the darkness, or command the center stage. As Angel, of course, the only thing he can't do is enjoy the daylight.

As David, he can live in the day. But he lives quietly. He might have been anointed as the new star of television, the hot hunk, yet he shies away from the glare, almost as if it could kill him. He has his dogs, and his wife, Ingrid, a social worker he dated for years before they married. He's not out on the town, alone or with her. The paparazzi aren't filing pictures of them at every party or every club. If David wants recreation, some time away, you won't find him prowling the night. Instead, he'll be on the golf course, enjoying a leisurely eighteen holes.

If he chooses not to be a star away from the screen, there's no denying that on it he's attracted a huge audience. According to *FHM* magazine, Buffy herself, Sarah Michelle Gellar, might be the sexiest woman in the world, but there are plenty of females who'd gladly vote for David as the sexiest man. For himself, he's quite honest and doesn't see what makes him so special.

"Am I a sex symbol?" he laughs. "I'd have to thank my mom and dad; they made me."

For him, it's about the acting. The chemistry of the performers on the show has been something special, and he can only hope it's repeated in *Angel*, which will team him with another *Buffy* veteran, Charisma Carpenter. She'll still be Cordelia, but a less snotty Cordelia than the one who wanted to be the queen of Sunnydale High.

From a modest start, *Buffy the Vampire Slayer* has grown to become much more than a cult show—for many it's appointment viewing, and every Tuesday night they'll gladly park themselves in front of the TV set for an hour to check out the latest events in Hellmouth. The actors on the show have become known, and publicly recognized. David has noted that such things tend to go with the territory, and that all you can do is accept it as it happens. Inevitably, as *Buffy* became more popular, more and more people would come up to him in public to tell him that they enjoy the show and the character. In some ways, he enjoyed being recognized, even when it could get a little crazy. And he had plenty to be proud of, doing strong work on an excellent show.

Unlike so many other actors, though, David hasn't used Angel as a starting point to rush into a movie career. Sarah Michelle Gellar and Seth Green might have been very active on movie sets during their vacations, but David is content to kick back, take Bertha Blue for a walk, maybe fit in a round of golf, spend time with Ingrid. He has his priorities, and they include time to himself, to come down from the intensity of working.

Not that he doesn't want a long career, or that he can't see Angel. But there's time for that, and he wants to only take parts he feels passionate about, something that matters to him, that moves him, not the very first thing he's offered. Too many television actors have seen themselves become sex symbols on the small screen, then tried to make a quick transition to movies, only to flop embarrassingly (David Caruso of *NYPD*, anyone?). If you live as a sex symbol, you die as one, and David wants to be taken more seriously than that. He's not just a pretty face; he's an actor, and that means creating a character.

Many of those watching the show might love David's looks, but in many ways it's the dark romance of Angel that moves then. There's a romance about the undead that has attracted people for many years. Maybe it's in the fact that vampires traditionally suck blood through a very seductive bite on the neck. Perhaps it's in the continued pursuit of new victims. Or perhaps it's in the idea of being able to live forever. Some take it more seriously than others; there have been cases where people have had their incisors filed to look like fangs, which is a far cry from the plastic fangs and black capes some kids don at Halloween.

The simple matter is that people are attracted to the dark side of things. It's a part of all our natures, although we tend to suppress it in our everyday lives. The myth of the vampire allows us to release that. We know—or at least most believe—that no such things as vampires exist. But the fiction of it lets us embrace our own dark sides quite safely, from a distance. And, since a crucifix can keep a vampire at bay, it also taps into the idea of God and the devil, good overcoming evil, as well as the triumph of Christianity over paganism.

Darkness seems to have been a theme in David's career—at least so far. His first professional acting job, in a commercial for Foster's beer, never saw the light of day, he says, because it was "too dark." Some things never change.

Angel, or Angelus, to give him his proper vampire name, is something of a contradiction in terms. He wreaked havoc all over Europe until a curse restored his soul and conscience. He tried to atone for his sins by helping humanity—and that included helping Buffy, the Slayer herself, kill vampires, his own kind. But nothing goes to plan—Angel and Buffy fell in love. Something that shouldn't have happened, did.

"Angel is a good guy in a bad situation," David explains about the character, "he's torn between two worlds and is in love with a girl who should kill him. Angel has a lot of passion he hasn't bitten into yet."

Puns aside, sleeping with Buffy lifted Angel's curse, and made him into a "real" vampire again. It was only a spell that restored his soul. He's literally been to hell and back. And now he broods. He has the heart of a human—a two-hundred-and-forty-three-year-old human—but the limits of a vampire. He lives in the night, in the shadows. He wants to be fully human, but he can never walk in the daylight (like all vampires); he can only think of the sun. His relationship with Buffy, once so close, so loving, has become . . . undefined. He lives a brooding existence. It can't be anything more. He helps when and where he can, but he's always out on the fringes.

". . . . what Angel would love to do more than anything is watch the sunrise with Buffy," David says. "He would love to possess some kind of special powers that let him go back into the sun, at least for a little bit."

That, of course, is impossible. But part of desire is

not always being able to attain it. If everything every-one desired came to pass, there'd be little to strive for. We want the things we can't have, to go back and erase the past, to reinvent ourselves, and to become people we can never be.

Angel has reinvented himself several times, over the course of several human lifetimes. He's lived the life of the highborn, traveled with tinkers and paupers. He's known the Master, the oldest vampire on record, and made love to the Slayer. He's added legions to the ranks of the undead, then turned around and helped eradicate his former brethren. He's the battle between good and evil, the light and the dark, that's in us all. Like all vampires, indeed like all mytholog-ical creatures, he's a symbol representing something about humanity.

He's become the ultimate loner, who can never be a member of one group or another. No longer a "proper" vampire, but unable to be completely human, he has no choice but to walk alone, constantly plagued by the memory of his killings, yet never able to fully atone for them. And the idea of the loner, the one who haunts the shadows, only adds to his romantic image.

The image of the vampire has changed drastically, and it's largely due to the influence of the movies. The Dracula of Bram Stoker's book, for example, was something truly evil, the stuff of nightmares. By the time of *Bram Stoker's Dracula*, Francis Ford Cop-pola's 1992 film, Gary Oldman portrayed the best-known vampire as a lonely, misunderstood soul who wanted nothing more than to be reunited with his dead love. For all that, he came across as hip, a person of presence and personality. Much the same was true of

Interview With The Vampire, where Brad Pitt and Tom Cruise glided through the centuries taking their pleasure; it was impossible to resist their charms. In fact, it was Anne Rice's book, from which the film was made, that seemed to renew the interest in vampires. For the first time, it gave real depth to their characters, something beyond wild eyes, fangs, blood, and coffins. Joss Whedon himself has said that he loved the book when he was younger "and Angel probably owes something to that." In fact, there are a few similarities between Brad Pitt's character, Louis, and Angel—both seem to share an introspection and compassion. Vampires with consciences and remorse.

Angel was born in Ireland, David far, far away in Buffalo, New York. They come together five days a week, when David reports to the set. Apart from that, they're two very different people. David is an actor—he's acted as long as he can remember—but his real aspiration was toward production—something he hopes to develop in the future. Television, and performing, has been around him his entire life. His father, Dave Roberts, is the weather forecaster for WPVI in Philadelphia, the city where David grew up. His sisters, Beth and Bo, both work behind the cameras, Beth as a production coordinator for *The Rosie O'Donnell Show* and Bo as a costumer for films. Indeed, David had no thoughts of acting professionally until he applied for crew work in Los Angeles, fresh from college with a degree in film, and found himself hired to be in front of the cameras. . . . but life always takes strange turns, and you have to go with the flow.

The flow seemed to be quite sluggish. There was a role in the Fox comedy *Married . . . with Children* followed by a handful of stage productions. And then there was *Buffy the Vampire Slayer*. He was the right person in the right place at the right time. Like so many things in show business—in life, for that matter—it came down to luck, backed up with talent. He got his break, and he's made it work.

From Buffalo to Philly, to Ithaca to Los Angeles, it's been a long trip to find home. But now, with Ingrid and Bertha Blue, as well as their other dog, a Chinese Crested, he has his place in the sun. He can play golf, he can stay home and read—he's an avid reader with a large library. The idea of celebrity, of being famous for fame's sake, holds no attraction for him. His head rests firmly on his shoulders. Life is for living, for enjoying, and that means working and being with his family. David Boreanaz doesn't need the darkness for his light.

CHAPTER ONE

BUFFALO,
New York, where David Boreanaz (to clarify, the
name is pronounced Bor-ee-ah-nuz, and it's of Czech
origin) was born, is a long way—geographically and
culturally—from Los Angeles, where he now lives.
It's the width of a continent, but also the span of several mindsets and climates. In Buffalo the winter cold
seizes hold and doesn't let go for months. Blizzards,
snowstorms, bitterly cold temperatures are the order
of each winter. Winter is a season that doesn't touch
L.A., a place where palm trees grow and the sun
shines with a rare intensity, even through the smog.
In Buffalo, the local dish is a pork and beef hot dog
cut and mashed in the grill until it becomes a tube
steak. In the City of Angels it's whatever the trendy
cuisine of the week might be, served up by a celebrity chef to celebrity guests. They're two different
worlds.

But David's story doesn't actually begin in Buffalo. It starts a couple of hundred miles away, in another country—Toronto, Canada, where, he says, he
was conceived. His father, who went by the name of
Dave Roberts—it played better than the more ethnic
Boreanaz—was an entertainer who played clubs and

theaters. It was a nomadic existence, really, but one
Roberts enjoyed—his only desire had been to entertain people. He traveled around the Northeast, which
included stints in Ontario and Quebec, making people laugh and smile. Sometimes his wife would ac-
company him, and the trips would seem more like
vacations than work. And she went with him to Toronto in August 1970, where the first intimations of
David Boreanaz became a twinkling in his parents'
eyes.

Home for the family, though, was Buffalo. Perhaps
it wasn't the most romantic city in the United States,
with more than its share of gritty reality, rather than
the open dreams of the West, but it suited them. They
were working people, even if Roberts's work was
somewhat different from being on the line in a factory
or pushing paper in an office.

David Boreanaz pushed his way into the world on
May 16, 1971, born under the sign of Taurus, the bull.
While Roberts was on the road, it was his wife Patti
who stayed home with David and his two sisters, Beth
and Bo. The three of them grew up with the idea of
performing as a completely natural part of life; they
saw it in their father every day—how could it be anything else but normal?

An entertainer's life was fine for a man with few
ties or responsibilities. But with three kids, Dave Roberts needed something that was a little more secure,
if he was going to provide well for his family. He
wanted to be around more, to watch his children grow,
to have something that seemed more stable. So when
he applied for—and won—the job of weather forecaster on Philadelphia television station WPVI in
Philadelphia, he was overjoyed. It meant a move, of

course, but that was fine. He'd have a job where he could be in front on the public, could entertain (he wasn't a meteorologist), and which was well paid. He'd be home every night. It was as if he'd been offered the perfect job.

Being a face on television meant that Roberts inevitably became something of a minor celebrity in Philadelphia. He was recognized on the street more than he'd ever been during his years as a traveling entertainer. A generous, outgoing man by nature, his attitude to the people who'd stop him had a deep effect on his son.

A lot of times when David was growing up he'd be out with his dad when fans would come up and say, "You're Dave Roberts!" His father acknowledged his fans enough to take the time to stop and talk to each one of those people, setting a solid example for David in later life.

Something else that David took from his father was performing. Although he probably couldn't really remember seeing him on stage often, somehow the idea was buried in him. Like his father, he wanted to perform.

That first came when David was four. With his own Rumplestiltskin Theater, he put on little plays at home for his family. Pictures of David back then show him with long, curly hair that was blond—the darker shade came in as he grew older.

A lot of kids put on plays for their families and friends; however, it doesn't necessarily mark them out as future actors. Besides, at four no one has a real sense of what they want to do with their lives. It's all play, as it should be, experimenting.

But not many kids find their vocation when they're

seven, either. David did. His moment of revelation came when his parents took him to see a revival of the musical *The King and I*, which saw the late Yul Brynner reprising his role as the King of Siam. It was a night that just hit him.

"I was in the third row, and I was just blown away by his performance," he remembers. "I just knew I wanted to be the king, I wanted to be an actor." Of course, there was a huge difference between a seven-year-old's idea of an actor and reality. Some would perhaps have pursued the goal immediately, trying to get children's roles on television, to be in commercials, or things of that nature. It didn't happen that way for David. His parents had enough experience of the business to know they didn't want that for their son—at least, not when he was young. If he still wanted to act when he was older, when his ideas were *real*, they'd happily support him. For now, though, what they wanted was for their kids to have a normal childhood. And that included time in the country, most specifically at a farm, where David developed the great fear of his life—chickens.

"I think I developed that fear when I was a little kid because I used to chase them at a farm and torment them and they would torment me. I must have been three or four."

Well, maybe not perfectly normal. There was no public school for the Boreanaz children. Dave and Patti wanted their kids to have the best education, the best start in life, that they could manage, and that meant the more exclusive prep school route. And why not? It was a perfectly natural impulse.

The obvious choice for David was Malvern Prep, probably the best-known preparatory school in Phila-

delphia, and one with a national reputation. It was a
place where David could have been involved in
school drama productions, but instead he preferred to
hide his light under a bushel—he was just another kid,
albeit one who was quite big and strong.

Size meant, inevitably, football, and David did play
on the team. And that, of course, meant that he was
labeled as a jock. But, like any pigeonhole, he didn't
fit neatly into a stereotype. Just because he wasn't
acting himself didn't mean that his love of theater had
vanished. Philadelphia wasn't far from New York,
and David would often go with his parents to see
stage productions.

"I was always around the theater in [New York],"
he says. "It grew on me as I grew older."

With its uniform (including a tie) and code for hair
length (David had no choice but to wear his short),
Malvern's aim was to turn out good citizens who'd
been well educated, and well prepared for college. It
was a school where the boys participated in things;
that was expected of them, the same way good grades
were the norm, not the exception. Parents were paying
for the best, and it was the school's job to deliver.

So David was a good kid. He studied hard, and
played football until his junior year, when he was in-
jured and had to quit. Every day he rubbed shoulders
with the sons of Philadelphia's moneyed elite, the kids
whose fathers were in business, politics, all sorts of
things. The one common factor was that they were all
successful, and most expected their children to be successful too. Straight teeth and good looks were common in the hallways. By the standards of most public
schools, the place was a dream. There were very few
disciplinary problems, the students all *wanted* to

achieve, and there was a real sense of school spirit. But things like that were the reason people paid a lot of money for their kids to attend Malvern.

Like most teenagers, David both belonged and stood outside from the different cliques. Playing football gained him entry to the group of jocks, even after his injury stopped him playing. But his love of theater was something that set him apart from all that, something he kept hidden for a long time, in the way boys often submerge their softer side, for fear of ridicule. But he did learn one important lesson—"I found that it's okay to cry. I had a big problem with that and I always thought if you cried you were a sissy and you were pushed away and teased." But he managed to get past that, and realized later it was a good thing.

Most kids strive for the grail of coolness, of being admired by their peers. To this day, David isn't sure if he managed it, or if he really cared. One of his idols was the Fonz, Arthur Fonzarelli, the leather-jacket-wearing cool character on the sitcom *Happy Days*. Whether David managed the same level of cool in his own life, he doesn't know. The most important thing is that he was happy with himself.

What was it about the stage, about creating roles and characters, that intrigued him? It was hard to say. Maybe just the act of doing it, of creating this illusion. In many ways it was the creating that captivated him, as much as the acting, all the steps involved in a production. The technical side was every bit as fascinating as the artistic side.

There were plenty of subjects he could have considered study at college. He was a bright student, well grounded and well liked. He'd made good grades all the way through school, and scored high in his

SATs. While any possibility of a football scholarship had fallen by the wayside, the academic field was wide open to him. But if he was going to attend college, it seemed to him that it should be to study a subject that truly interested him; otherwise he'd simply be going through the motions, and there was no point in that. And so, in his senior year, he sent out his college applications to study film.

For someone so enthusiastic about live drama it seemed an odd, even unlikely choice. Yet there was a certain logic to it. There were far more jobs in movies and television than there were in the theater. It was a field that was expanding, where someone with a degree and a good background could find work— or so he believed. He'd certainly thought the whole thing through.

His original intention was to get a job on the production side of the business and work behind the camera, rather than in front of it. He loved the whole process, the preparation of both film and television. While television, he noted, had a much quicker turn-around time, film took longer, but the actual process of making a movie was more satisfying. They were both art forms, but of two different kinds, the difference being somewhat like the difference between watercolors and oil painting—separate but equal.

It's possible that the careers of his sisters had some influence on his decision, too. Both of them worked in movies and television. Bo, the older, was a costumer, whose credits included *Barton Fink* and *Escape From L.A.*, while Beth had gone into television, working as a production coordinator on *The Rosie O'Donnell Show*. None of the Boreanaz acorns had fallen too far from the tree; to a greater or lesser degree, show business seemed to be in their blood.

At that time, the idea of acting for a living wasn't in David's mind. He knew full well all the trials and tribulations it would involve, and all the sacrifice. Most actors never made a living. They hustled for parts, even small parts. It was much better—and much more secure—being on the other side of the camera. He admired the actor's art, but somehow he couldn't see himself doing it. While for many, acting was mostly about a "look" he knew there was much more involved.

Even on his graduation—he graduated early, in 1987—David was a good-looking boy. He hadn't really grown into his face yet, but the heartthrob was already there. The face didn't have the same brooding quality, and his hair was curlier, but it was still unmistakably David Boreanaz.

There weren't that many schools with good film programs. NYU had a strong reputation, and New York was close to Philadelphia, almost commuting distance. But what David needed was somewhere far enough away to really seem "away," where he could be off on his own, to grow. And the answer came in the form of Ithaca College, in New York. Located in the center of the state, some forty miles from the Pennsylvania state line (but a good distance from Philly), it was a prestigious private school—which translated into costly.

Ithaca was one of the colleges to which David applied, and they were happy to accept someone with his record and SAT scores. His future—at least the next four years of it—was set out.

*   *   *

After the big-city life of Philadelphia, Ithaca was something of a shock for David. It was a college town, with fewer than thirty thousand full-time residents, although that population swelled during the academic year. Apart from Ithaca College, the city was also home to Cornell University, an institution with a long and proud history.

Although, in real terms, Ithaca wasn't too far from anywhere (Syracuse, for example, was only forty miles away), it remained fairly isolated in the Finger Lakes area of central New York state. There weren't going to be too many distractions from learning (unless, of course, you counted partying).

Ithaca College itself had been founded in 1892, although back then it was the Ithaca Conservatory of Music. It quickly gained a strong reputation, and by the 1930s boasted more than two thousand students. The change to a full university happened over the next couple of decades, although the college remained on its downtown campus until the 1960s, when a new, purpose-built campus was erected in the South Hill area of town, away from the center, overlooking Cayuga Lake.

It was a lovely area, a planner's dream, green and airy. The buildings were modern but still authoritative.

As a private school, Ithaca College kept admission low—even today there are fewer than six thousand students—to allow a much better student-to-teacher ratio; in Ithaca's case, it currently stands at 12:1, astonishingly low by the standards of most universities. That meant the education was more personalized, and professors had a chance to really know their students, which worked to everyone's advantage. It was geared mostly to the four-year undergraduate program, with very few graduate students pursuing advanced degrees. The biggest plus, in David's case, was that the film program at Ithaca was nationally acknowledged as one of the best.

Prep school had instilled a strong work ethic in him, and he brought that with him to New York. David had never been one to spend his free time partying his brains out. Excess simply wasn't a part of his nature. He understood full well that his parents were paying a lot of money for his education, and he wanted to make sure they got full value. Let the others waste every penny and waste four years of their lives; he was there to learn.

That didn't mean he became a complete recluse or some kind of film nerd. He was still the sociable person he'd always been. But, freed from the pressure to conform that had existed at Malvern Prep, he could be much more himself—somewhat introspective, someone who was happy to stay in his dorm room and read a book when he wasn't completing an assignment. He made friends, had girlfriends, but to most he was an anonymous figure on campus. The injury he'd suffered in his junior year at school had ended any football prospects, and that had always been his main sport. So now he simply blended into the pleasant scenery at Ithaca, worked hard, and maintained good grades.

He'd never rebelled against his parents, or gone through those years of teen angst. He'd been luckier than many, inasmuch as his parents had always encouraged him to do what *he* wanted to do, rather than mindlessly conform. And they'd always been supportive of his decisions. There'd been little for him to rebel against, really. So he went off to college quite well adjusted, his feet firmly on the ground, with a very clear vision of what he wanted to do in life, and the amount of work it would take to achieve that.

David had never been a film obsessive in the way many of the other students in his film class were (think Dawson on *Dawson's Creek*). He didn't need—and didn't want—to be able to quote chapter and verse on almost every movie ever made. What he wanted was to learn the production end of films, to understand, and to develop the art he sensed was inside himself. He didn't need to be a walking encyclopedia of the movies in order to do that.

At the same time, some knowledge of film history was necessary, and that was a part of his course, along with all the other, more technical, aspects. He took it all in, completing all his courses on a strong, if not spectacular, level.

Every vacation would mean home to Philadelphia, and a chance to get together with his family. They were close, the type to stand up for each other, no matter what, and David had learned to value that. He still lists his father, and his grandfather (whom he calls "an unbelievable wise man, full of knowledge") as his heroes.

Of course, college brought changes for David. He was growing, in every possible way. And that meant experimentation. He let his hair grow long, in what he called his "Deadhead" phase (after the band, Grateful Dead), and wore all the appropriate hippie gear. When that became old, he cut his locks short again. But somehow it didn't work; his hair struck out oddly, and he found himself stuck with the nickname Q-Tip Head—not exactly the sort of handle anyone wants to go by. So he shaved the side of his head, hoping that would tame his hair.

He also attempted to pierce his left ear by himself, something that didn't work too well.

"It got infected," he remembers, "and I got this huge bubble behind my ear. I had to go to the emergency room to get it lanced."

But it was college, the time in your life when you're supposed to be able to do that kind of thing, to try on ideas, personalities, hairstyles, and clothes. While not on the curriculum, that's part of the overall education, a chance to learn who you really are—and who you're not.

Certainly David found out who—and what—he wasn't. He wasn't really a latter-day hippie. He wasn't a punk. And trying to stand out from the crowd simply physically disagreed with him. He was at his happiest being ordinary, looking "normal," like himself. That was who he was at heart, where he felt most comfortable. He tried to try other things to understand that. He could look like other people and still be himself; it didn't make him into a sheep, a follower. He still had his personal likes and dislikes that had absolutely nothing to do with any fashion—particularly when it came to music: "I'm very old school," he admits. "I'm a huge Dead Head. I like the Rolling Stones and Bob Dylan." You didn't have to look the part to feel the part was the obvious lesson. You could just be yourself.

There was no shortage of girls interested in him. He was six feet one, broad-shouldered and buff, and he had the dark good looks that are now his trademark. He dated, but there was no one special. College, for him, was more about studying and learning—

about film, about himself—than for anything else.

Like most students, he spent all four of his years there living in the dorms. In Ithaca, apart from the frat houses, there weren't many other choices. And it made his life simpler, to be catered to, not to have to think of his own cooking and grocery shopping, all the chores that would come soon enough, anyway. He was focused, and happy to be attending class, taking care of all his assignments.

And that was the way it went until 1991, when he graduated. There was little to distinguish David from the pack in terms of academics. He was good, not great. He worked hard, and donned his cap and gown in the June heat to accept his diploma. He'd spent sixteen years studying in order to reach this point, applying himself every day.

But he knew a degree in film wasn't a passport to success of any kind. It might help open a few doors— after that, he was on his own. Every year thousands of people graduated with film degrees and tons of ambition. And most of them did what he planned to do— head west, to Los Angeles, and try to find work.

At least he had a realistic attitude. He knew his degree didn't make him the new Scorsese. He understood that whatever work he got would be at the bottom of the heap. He wasn't going to walk into the movies or television and immediately start directing or producing. There was a little more security in a job behind the cameras than in front, but not a whole lot. Yet this was what he wanted to do with his life. This was the pull he'd felt for years, and now it was about to become reality. It wasn't going to be easy. It wasn't even going to be a sure thing. But it was what he had to do, he knew that. If he failed, well, at least he'd tried. At this point it was all up to him, and somehow that was a comforting feeling; he had confidence in himself.

CHAPTER TWO

GO

West, young man, has been the American creed almost since the first white settlers arrived. West was land, West was fortune and opportunity. And California, more than anywhere else, has represented that, ever since the Gold Rush of 1849. It was a place you could get rich, a state where anything was possible. Once the movie industry set up shop in Hollywood in the early years of the twentieth century, it became a magnet for people with ideas, people with looks, with acting skills. Movies offered fame on a scale few could have imagined. They went around the world, making a select few into massive international stars.

The start of television also brought stardom, and the need for programming—lots of programming—to fill the evenings, then the days. That meant more jobs, more possibilities. If you had a look, if you could act, if you had any type of production skills, Los Angeles was the place to be. Even if you didn't have any of those talents, but you could hustle, L.A. offered plenty of opportunities for you.

For David, with his degree in film, Los Angeles wasn't so much the obvious choice as the only one. After graduation, he'd sat and discussed his plans with his parents. They understood that this wasn't simply the wild pursuit of a dream, it was what he needed to follow his chosen career. L.A. was where the film work was, and that was where David needed to be. But that didn't mean they were about to let their son just vanish there alone. Instead, David's father took some time off work, and arranged to drive out there with him. Not only would the trip be more lively that way, he could also see that David was settled into a decent place, and that everything was taken care of to his satisfaction. It was a bonding time for father and son, right before the son struck out on his own. The boy might have been grown, but parents never let go.

No one said it would be easy. There was no job waiting for him. He was one of hundreds of hopefuls arriving in Los Angeles every week. Granted, with a film degree from a prestigious school he had some advantages, but it was still going to mean starting at the bottom of the technical pile—once he got a job. If he got in, he'd be able to build on that. But getting in would be the trick.

After Dave Roberts had reassured himself that his son would be fine, that he wouldn't starve to death or be homeless, he headed back to Philadelphia, leaving David to explore and find his feet in a strange city. And, more important, to get out his resumes and start seriously hunting for some work.

He was lucky. Within a few weeks he'd found a job as a prop master on a shoot for a commercial. When the call came, David thought he was on his way. What he didn't know was that the way was about to take a strange turn. When he reported to the set, there was some confusion. This guy was the *prop master*? How come he wasn't one of the actors?

He didn't have a clue what was happening. He simply expected to be doing what he'd been hired to do, and suddenly there was the director and people from the ad agency wanting him to be in front of the camera; it was confusing. But the money was far more than he would have earned as prop master, that was for sure.

When it happened, it struck David as something completely bizarre, but he went along with it; the money was useful, and turning down anything at this stage would be foolish. But when it happened for a *second* time on another job, he realized something was happening here.

He had, he said, actually gone along to apply for work on the crew; that was his experience. But instead he was cast as an actor, not a technician. The first onscreen job he had was in a commercial for Foster's beer, although in the end it never aired, being deemed "too dark."

You might well say that David's first screen appearance was something of a portent for the major role ahead of him, but that wouldn't be fair. At that point no one could have known. Indeed, when it happened, in 1992, the original movie version of *Buffy the Vampire Slayer*, with Kristy Swanson in the title role, and a very different vision of the idea (although still from the pen of Joss Whedon), was just appearing in theaters.

It was as if forces outside himself were telling David that his future was in front of the cameras, something he'd never anticipated. Stardom wasn't something he'd sought. He was quite happy to be anonymous, a guy doing something he loved. But he knew enough to understand that when Fate comes calling, you can't refuse her.

"You define your existence by being truthful to yourself," he says, and in this case, there was only one truth. Everything was propelling him back to acting. He had no choice, no say in the matter. When he was younger he'd acted for his family. Now David Boreanaz, the actor, was being reborn.

It was a strange feeling. He'd been so certain of his future. Now, even though he was only twenty-two, the career he'd mapped out had already been derailed. He was meant to act. He'd been born to act. And that meant he had to understand more about acting.

He learned a great deal in the same way he'd always learned things—he read a lot. There were plenty of texts out there, written by people with names like Stanislavsky, full of ideas and theories, and he digested them whole.

At the same time, he knew that he could have all the talent in the world, but if no one knew he was around it wouldn't do him any good. He needed to be noticed. People needed to be aware that he was around and available. Without credits or connections it was hard to find an agent. Without an agent it was hard to get an acting job. It was a vicious circle. He needed to break it. And the best way to do that was to be as businesslike—and un-actor-like—as possible.

"I'd put on a suit and pretend I was an executive just to get into studio lots," he remembers. "I'd pass out resumes and talk to people. I was in this one agency, and I had security chasing me around the building."

It wasn't the way he wanted to get into (or be forced to leave) the studios, but you had to do what you could. Whether anyone would remember him, and whether anyone would actually read his resume, was doubtful. But at least he'd made an attempt, he'd done what was in his power to do.

But he also had to feed himself and pay rent on his apartment. Something was compelling him toward acting, but until he started working, there was no money coming in from it. And that meant he had to start looking for work elsewhere. Not a career, any kind of job he couldn't just walk away from for a good audition or to take a role. Just work. Something with a paycheck to keep body and soul together.

That translated into what was essentially menial work. And it would be a good three years before he'd be able to move on from it. But he always tried to make the best of the situation and try to enjoy himself.

His philosophy was that eventually he'd be acting for a living, that these jobs wouldn't last long, so he might as well enjoy them. There were times it wasn't easy, but he managed to make the best of it.

And, of course, he was auditioning for everything he could. Even when he didn't get the role—which was virtually all the time—the experience was good. It forced him to learn and sharpen his skills. And some work as an extra did come his way. He appeared in two movies, *Aspen Extreme* and *Best of the Best II*. He received no credit in either film, but they were a first foot on the ladder. If nothing else, he'd proved that his appearance in the commercials wasn't a fluke. There was a future for him as an actor.

Videohound's Golden Movie Retriever doesn't have many kind words for *Aspen Extreme*. There were no familiar names in the cast of the movie, which was written and directed by Patrick Hasburgh, himself a former Aspen ski instructor, and set in—where else—Aspen. Strangely, though, both the leads would go on to bigger things: Paul Gross made his mark in the television series *Due South*, and Peter Berg became a leading member of the *Chicago Hope* cast. Whatever glimpses there were of David were, at best, very brief; in fact, you'd be hard pressed to even notice him at all.

The same was true of *Best of the Best II*, a martial arts film that didn't exactly score rave reviews. Starring Eric Roberts and Christopher Penn, with appearances by Wayne Newton and Meg Foster, it was directed by Robert Radler, and largely sank without a trace upon its release in 1993.

On top of that, David did appear in another film, *Eyes of the World*, whose fate was even worse than the other two—it wasn't released at all, not even on video.

One thing was for sure—David wasn't going to support himself by working as an extra. He knew that full well, and kept pushing away, auditioning for everything, trying to get an agent. At the same time, he wanted a life. While forging ahead was important, acting wasn't the sole thing in life. He had other interests.

"I like to be outside. . . ." he says. "I like hiking, mountain biking, traveling." While traveling was off the agenda for right now, there was time for the other things, to keep a balance going. He was adamant about maintaining that, making time to listen to music, to get out of the house, to know that he wasn't spending all his time working either dead-end jobs or trying for something as an actor. It was a way of keeping sane.

While his real aim was television or movies, which was where the money and most of the work in Los Angeles was, he knew that the best way to hone his skills was simply to act—and that meant on the stage. While not a great town for live theater, L.A. did offer some opportunities in that department. And every production meant another line on his resume. With the Ensemble Theatre, he took part in *Hatful of Rain*, and then *Italian-American Reconciliation* and *Fool for Love*, both on the Gardner Stage.

For any actor, David advocated doing as much stage work as possible. It was the chance to get up in front of an audience and work that gave an actor a chance to become more confident about his abilities, and the chance to make mistakes, to have them work and learn from them. It was akin to a baby learning to walk, falling down, then getting up again doing it some more until it was happily running.

But what David didn't point out is that you have to have the talent to act in the first place. Many people want to, but few are really able to make a character come alive from a script. It's something innate. Technique can be learned, but without that talent, there's never a vibrancy to it. It's what separates community theater from the professionals. And David has that innate talent, as anyone who's seen him on *Buffy* can definitely testify. It's something that can't be put into words. Presence is a part of it, but it's not the whole thing. It's the way an actor can make the character believable, make an audience suspend its disbelief and feel as if this person really and truly exists.

It was satisfying on an artistic level to perform on a stage, and all excellent experience. But it wasn't making him famous or wealthy—it wasn't even raising him above the poverty line as an actor. What David needed was a break. . . .

CHAPTER THREE

THE kind of break David needed could have been almost anything, as long as it got him noticed. A speaking part in some program which would show that he could act would have been ideal. To say he thought about it often would have been something of an understatement. When he was painting houses or working in valet parking at the Beverly Wilshire Hotel—one place where he could constantly see celebrities who'd made it—there wasn't much else to think about. The jobs didn't require much brain power, simply being there.

He was still making the rounds with his resume, which had, at least, grown a little. And he was still enthusiastically attending every audition he could. While he knew in his head that Los Angeles was full of unemployed actors, though, the frustration of trying and trying and hardly making any headway was frustrating. To know you have the talent to do something, but never being given the opportunity, would wear on anyone.

But David had never been a quitter. He'd succeeded at everything he'd tried, and he was determined that acting would not be the exception. His belief in himself remained strong, and his determination was powerful. He wanted a break, and he'd keep working until he made it happen.

Sometimes luck can run someone's way, and in Hollywood luck can be an important factor, being in the right place at the right time. In 1993, luck smiled briefly on David. He auditioned for a role on a television sitcom—and won it! Finally, he thought, he was starting to make some headway.

The sitcom was *Married . . . with Children*, on the Fox network. It had been around since the network's inception, one of their mainstays and top-rated shows. The humor tended to be outrageous, and it made no attempt to seek out a highbrow audience. It had also launched the career of one of the sex symbols of the nineties, Christina Applegate, who played the daughter of the Bundy family, Kelly.

In the episode known as the "Movie Show," David would be playing Kelly's new boyfriend, Frank. Frank was a biker, a tough guy in a leather jacket—the sort that would have been called a hood a couple of generations before.

It wasn't exactly a big part. But not all parts were. You did whatever you could with the material that was available. Kelly had to break a date with Frank so her parents could take her out to a movie for her birthday. At the theater, Kelly would see Frank with another girl, and Frank would find himself in the unlikely situation of being beaten up by Al Bundy—not exactly one of television's hard cases.

"*Married . . . with Children* was a laugh," David recalls. As he pointed out, taping a sitcom in front of a live audience was very similiar to performing in live theater—although there was the chance to replay a scene that wasn't perfect.

More important, it gave him exposure. Millions of people tuned in to the show every week, and had the chance to see David. He looked good, there was no doubt about that. Even then, the looks and brooding aspect that would come to the fore in Angel were there—just not developed.

It would be hard to call his appearance a few minutes of fame. On *Married . . . with Children*, Kelly Bundy changed boyfriends the way most people changed socks; Frank was just one in a long line. A few minutes on-camera for David. There would be no more guest shots, no chance to develop the character. He was there primarily as a foil for Al Bundy, not as a complete character.

But you took what was offered, and that was the best offer he'd had to date. It might not have been much, but at least David could say he'd been on national television now. And it all added to his resume. It was some money in the bank, and an attempt at something different—he'd never played comedy before.

Would anyone remember him from the show? The truth, and he knew it himself, was probably not. He was just another face with a few brief lines of dialogue. It was fun rehearsing and taping, but once it was over, it was forgotten. It didn't bring casting agents knocking down his door. In truth, it didn't seem to do a thing for his career. That was the way of things, though; David understood that. It was *a* break. That didn't mean it was *the* break. He'd made some headway. He'd been on a network show. If he could do it once, he could do it again and again. All it required, apart from talent (and looks helped) was persistence. And he had plenty of that.

Still, national television had to count for something. Many entered the acting profession, but few made it even that far. It was a feather in his cap. Once it was over, it was back to the mundane ritual of daily work, however. The jobs changed with stunning regularity. For a while he drove around, emptying portable toilets—surely one of the worst jobs anyone could have—and for two weeks he and a friend drove around with a freezer truck selling meat door-to-door, until the friend went and locked the keys in one of the ice chests. He handed out towels at one of the many gyms where the Hollywood elite and wannabes kept themselves trim and buff. It was all soulless work (apt for a vampire, perhaps), it paid the bills, and left him time to concentrate on his art.

There was no doubt that David felt alone, though. He had friends, but not too many, and there was no steady girlfriend. He needed a companion. He needed a. . . . dog. That was when he found Bertha in the animal shelter. A mix of Labrador, German Shepherd, and greyhound, she was a mutt—but one he found instantly lovable. There was an immediate bond between them. With one ear cocked up, the other falling flat, she had a slightly tattered look that appealed to David. She was big and energetic. She was exactly what he needed and he took her home.

Now he had an even greater reason to get outside, to go for long walks, to roam in Griffith Park (the park with the observatory first made famous in the James Dean film *Rebel Without A Cause*). She was an independent dog, one who'd become quite used to going her own way, and saw no reason to change just because she now had a human around her. She didn't sleep in the house; instead, she had her own doghouse in the backyard, and that was the way she wanted it. Sometimes, when David let her off the leash in a park, she wouldn't come back. The first few times, he panicked, thinking he'd lost her. But one way or another, Bertha and David would find their way to each other.

Even though she's often been lost, she almost always found her way back home again, or David has found her when he's been out searching. Naturally, Bertha has a collar and tags with her name and David's phone number. She's an independent dog who needs a little time alone. And David, being David, has learned not to let her disappearances stress him out; she'll be back with him in due course. It's karma.

There was one instance when it did seem as if they might have been parted forever. They'd been in Griffith Park, and Bertha took off. David couldn't find her. He spent most of the day looking, then had to give up. Next day he was back, then the next, before realizing that she was truly gone. Six weeks passed, and he come to terms with the fact that she wasn't coming home again. He was sad, empty at the prospect of life without Bertha. Then a package arrived in the mail—her leash and collar. That meant she was alive somewhere—and with someone. Immediately David took out ads in the local papers, and hoped.

The people who had found her and taken her in contacted him. After some negotiations, Bertha came home again. The people who'd adopted her had named her Blue, and that was now added to her name—Bertha Blue.

Bertha Blue was as close to a constant companion as David had ever had. She was more than his dog;

she was his best friend, his confidante, and he took
what steps he could to make sure she would never
disappear from his life for extended periods. He knew
that the bond between them meant they were supposed to be together. But she valued her indepen-
dence, her time alone; sometimes she needed to
vanish for a little while, and David to learn to adapt
to that.

As he said, he didn't stress over it. He'd learned to
trust her, and to trust himself. But David didn't stress
over a great deal. What was meant to happen, would
happen. With Bertha Blue, it was like that old adage:
If you love something, set it free; if it comes back to
you, it's yours.

He kept that attitude to his career. He pushed as
much as he could, but he wasn't losing sleep over not
getting bigger parts yet. He had the faith it would happen. If that took a while, well, he had patience as well
as perseverance. All things come to him who waits. In
between, there were jobs, some good, some bad, to fill
his days, along with the auditions, and making the
rounds, passing out his resume. Weekends he could
take off with Bertha Blue, get out of town where the
air was cleaner, and they could have fun. In the evenings there was the occasional pickup basketball
game. He could go and play golf, a relaxing eighteen
holes on a public course. He could go bowling—a re-
cent favorite of his. In quieter moments, there were
books—the bookcases in his house were always
crammed to overflowing—or music, going back over
his beloved Grateful Dead, or the Stones . . . virtually
always something older.

It made for a full and rewarding life. It was balanced. Angst had never been David's way, even when
he was a teenager. He had a knack of being able to

take things in his stride, to absorb experiences and learn from them, to always find something positive in them. That put him ahead of a lot of people. Unlike Angel, brooding wasn't his thing. David certainly wasn't the type to live his life in the shadows, to be more observer than participant. He wanted to be out there, doing things he enjoyed. But he also understood the value of things coming together in the fullness of time—a trait he did share with his future alter ego.

It was just as well he did feel that way, because 1994 and 1995 were very barren years for David in the acting profession. The only lights he saw were on the stage, in productions of *A Hatful of Rain, Fool for Love*, and *Italian-American Reconciliation* (which must have appealed to him, given his mother's Italian-American background). Although he was fairly certain there wouldn't be a director or casting agent in the audience just looking for someone like him, he took all his parts very seriously, preparing very carefully for each role, and each performance, working long hours, in rehearsal and at home to make everything perfect.

He didn't practice in front of a mirror, the way some actors did, but he'd developed his own techniques for rehearsing a role, although he wasn't about to reveal them all; some things he needed to keep to himself, and that was important. He could do the same as any actor, take his script home and memorize all his lines. But that was only the beginning. You had, he pointed out, to start bringing the character alive at that point. So you tried things at home, or in rehearsal. Some the director would like, some he wouldn't—but you had to keep trying. Acting was a constant struggle to improve the character, to bring him more and more alive—at least it was for David. However good he was in a role, he always wanted to be better. Like any real artist, he was never truly satisfied with his work. However exhausting it might, the end result was always worth the effort.

For someone who came to acting late, and who'd never been formally trained, David's reading and his experience had helped him develop strong theories about the craft. But that was the way it should be; it showed he was taking it all very seriously, which was right, given that he was devoting his life, and his ambition, toward it.

Unlike television or film, a stage production takes place as a whole. It goes from beginning to end with no stops, no chances for a retake if someone messes up a line. For actors, as some have said, it's like working without a safety net—and that causes both thrills and fear in performers. You have to be on top of things, aware of what's going on. When it fails, it can be the worst feeling in the world—it's not for nothing that people talk about "dying" on stage. But when it works, and the actors spark off each other, it can be one of the most exhilarating experiences possible. And that is what everyone strives for, in every single performance of every play. When they've done it once, they want it again and again. When they achieve it, they know they have the audience with them. They can take chances, do whatever they choose, and sense the electricity in the air, the sense of history and memories being made. It's a feeling no television program or movie can ever duplicate, simply because there's no feedback between audience and cast. And that's what makes live theater so special for so many actors.

Stage acting gave David a chance to hone his craft.

Every night of a play's run was something different. It brought new problems, but also new opportunities, chances to try things, to hone things, to make himself into a better actor. Every performance was a learning experience for him. One thing was beyond doubt—he was a natural. He possessed that special something that couldn't be taught. And acting simply felt *right* to him; it was the thing he was supposed to be doing. It excited and comforted him at the same time.

If there was one big difficulty, it was that there simply weren't enough plays in which he could be involved. Television and film might have been his real goals—if he'd been truly dedicated to live theater he'd have made his home in New York, not Los Angeles—but in the meantime this kept him sharp, made him think about everything he was doing, and helped him constantly improve.

Married . . . with Children had given him one small break, but he'd been unable to capitalize on it. Hollywood was full of hunks, some even better-looking than David, even if most couldn't act as well as he did. Being there and trying to make it was like a crap shoot—a lot of it came down to luck, rather than talent. One day, he knew, he'd be in the right place at the right time, and things would go his way; that much was karma.

So in the meantime he worked his jobs, did everything he could, and made sure that his life was in balance. On the weekends he and Bertha Blue would seek out some fresh air and take their minds off everything that had happened the week before. A new week would mean new challenges—and also new possibilities. If he wasn't making it in Hollywood, David wasn't about to let that fact depress him. There was a great deal to be thankful for.

Still, he'd have had to be more than human not to sometimes wonder why it was taking so long. Like all actors, he had to have that unflagging confidence in his own abilities, and the fact that he *would* make it. But he'd been out on the West coast for a long time now. Little things had happened, enough to keep him simmering. But when would it all hit boiling point? The question must have come into his mind from time to time, when he felt low, or when he woke in the middle of the night and wondered exactly what he was doing there, questioning his choices as everyone does from time to time. But if he let good sense prevail, and let his patience take command, then it would all come right in the end. He just had to keep on hanging in there.

Above all, he didn't want to try and make himself into someone he wasn't, simply in order to try and pursue fame. Something was meant to be, and it would come to *him*, not some image. He'd tried once before to be something he wasn't, back in school when he pierced his ear, and he'd ended up in the hospital then. It was a lesson he'd taken to heart.

Eventually something good had to come his way. He just didn't know it would be *as good* as Angel.

Of course, it was all pure chance. And it was only reasonable that Bertha Blue should have had a hand in it, too; after all, she was a part of him and of his fortunes, good and bad. Whatever the weather, Bertha needed her walks. And David was happy to oblige. He loved being outside, even if the air in L.A. was smoggy, the pollution sometimes so thick it almost seemed as if it could have been cut by a knife. They'd walk for hours. It was therapy of sorts for David after working all day in a job that meant nothing to him. He could let his thoughts wander. And Bertha, being a big, athletic dog, was happy to keep going as long and as far as David wanted; he'd tire before she did.

So the two of them would explore neighborhoods, just go wherever they pleased, for miles at a time. Los Angeles is a massive, sprawling place. They already knew their immediate neighborhood well, and tended to roam far beyond it.

That was exactly what they were doing on that fateful day in the spring of 1996. David wasn't thinking about much, just strolling along, Bertha tugging at the leash, moving from smell to smell, examining everything in that canine way. They were on a residential street full of nice homes—maybe not the millionaire compounds of Beverly Hills or Bel Air, but still expensive. David hadn't even considered the people who might be living behind the windows. He was simply out for the exercise, enjoying the weather and Bertha Blue's company. He wasn't dressed to impress anyone. He was relaxed, unwinding.

Suddenly, at a house they'd just passed, the door opened and a man came out, walking rapidly. David didn't pay it any mind at first, until it became obvious that the man was walking toward him, and looking at him.

The obvious reaction was to believe this man imagined Bertha had done something to—or on—his front lawn, although David knew that wasn't the case. But the man didn't look angry; quite the opposite. And he wanted to talk.

He was, it transpired, a manager—more specifically, a manager of actors. And in David's face alone, he saw potential. That David was an actor was something he almost didn't need to ask. He was young, he was good-looking and buff, he was in L.A.—what else could he be? They chatted for a few minutes, then the manager invited David, and Bertha, into his house to talk business. It was fate—what else could David do but agree?

What the manager wanted was to sign David as one of his clients. That didn't mean a guarantee of work, or any kind of stardom. But he did know of a part that he believed would suit David perfectly. He had the look, the build, and the aura for it. It was on a new television series, so it might end up failing. At the same time, it could become a huge success; that was the gamble you took in this business, as David was well aware. If David was his client, he could arrange an audition.

It was a perfect Hollywood moment, the kind you read about, but which all too rarely happens. It was Lana Turner being "discovered" at the counter of Schwab's drugstore and being made into a star. It was everything exaggerated and dramatic, exactly the way it should be. And even if it failed, it would make a great story to retell later.

Of course, David wanted to be sure that the manager was legitimate, that this wasn't some bizarre scam. But once he was convinced of that, as he sat in the manager's living room with Bertha Blue curled at his feet, David knew that somehow this was very right. It was all too strange, too much of a coincidence, to be anything else. So he followed his instincts and signed a management contract. At least there was now someone else who wanted a hand in his career; part of the load for that had been taken off him.

The manager told him to go home, that he'd be hearing from him later in the day. David believed that, in part because he wanted to, but also because there was no reason why his new manager should lie. After all, his resume wasn't exactly bulging with credits. Unless there was some specific reason, there was no point in someone taking an interest in him. So he and Bertha jogged back to David's house, and he sat there, reading and waiting for the phone to ring.

The manager proved to be as good as his word. Within a couple of hours he was on the line. David had an audition the following morning. In the best Hollywood tradition, the script was being messengered over to him even as they spoke. All he had to do was learn the marked passages and be prepared to read.

The messenger came and went, and David was holding a partial script in his hands. He had to read for the character of Angel, whoever that was. He sat down, opened the pages, and began to look at it all.

In a way, it was completely overwhelming. To go from nothing to this within just a few hours. Sure, he didn't have the job yet, but no one would be going to this much trouble unless he had a good shot at it. This, he knew inside, was exactly the thing he'd been waiting for. His patience and perseverance were going to pay off—finally.

CHAPTER FOUR

THE audition, of course, was for *Buffy the Vampire Slayer*, and the role was that of Angel. What David didn't know was that the casting director, Marcia Shulman, was becoming quite desperate in her hunt for someone to play the part. She'd seen so many actors it had gone beyond funny. There were times she wondered if every male actor under the age of thirty had tried for Angel.

There was another factor too—time. There was literally one more day before Angel's scenes in the first episode were due to be filmed. Shulman needed the perfect Angel, and she needed him now. So, when she received the call from David's new manager, to say she was thrilled would have been putting it mildly. She arranged to see him the next morning and crossed her fingers that he was as good as the manager said, that it wasn't all just hype on behalf of his new client.

She needn't have worried. What she's been told didn't violate any truth in advertising laws. David came into the office and sat down. The first thing Shulman did was write on the casting sheet, 'He's the guy'—before she even heard him speak. Once he started to talk, she became totally convinced.

"I think what might have gotten me the role, actually, was the sense of humor I brought to the character," David assesses. "At the beginning of the audition, I was trying to turn the rocking chair into a motorcycle and got everybody laughing." It was a good start, and he'd passed the audition with Shulman. But that was just the first of his hurdles that day. He had to read for several other people, including the creator and writer of the series, Joss Whedon, who agreed with Shulman's assessment.

"We didn't have a lot of money, and he didn't have a lot of credits, so we were able to get him for cheap." Whedon laughs. There was one more thing that put the decision beyond any doubt, Whedon adds: "And, after the audition, all the women were shaking. We were lucky in that he also turned out to be an incredibly talented actor."

David himself had no idea how big the size of the character would become. All he was told was that Angel would be a recurring character in the first few episodes, and he took the job because "I just wanted to feed my dog." And, of course, because it was meant to be. Until he won the role, no one told him he needed to be on the set the following day, ready to work. There was none of the Hollywood wait and wait and wait for something to happen. He had to go straight from first gear into overdrive. And because of the speed with which things were moving, no one had a chance to explain much about the show to him.

"Because it happened so quickly, I hardly knew anything about the show," he recalls. "I didn't even have a full script, just the eight pages that Angel was on and I was shooting the day after I was cast. I didn't get to read the script until after work."

The idea of the recurring, peripheral character in a series was hardly new. And David had the looks to play the dark, mysterious stranger—who exactly was Angel, anyway?—to perfection. In real life he might have been open and often funny, but he could switch to brooding mode in an instant, and simply smolder on the set. It certainly didn't hurt that the camera seemed to love him, and brought out that innate hunkiness.

The first two episodes, which introduced all the main players, had Angel very much on the sidelines, the one who seemed to stand outside everything. He wasn't a Watcher like Giles, that much was for sure, but he seemed to know when bad things were going to happen. He wasn't a Slayer; Slayers were always female. And, being older and not in high school, he definitely wasn't one of the Slayerettes (the term was coined by Willow). He knew things, but stayed away from the action.

And what could anyone make of the chemistry between Angel and Buffy? The screen sizzled when they were together, right from the scene where she heard footsteps behind her and turned to find. . . . Angel. She was intrigued by him, but also somehow repulsed—she didn't know exactly what to think, other than there was definitely something there.

What had originally been intended as the first two episodes of *Buffy* were combined into one two-hour episode to introduce the series with a bang—and a bite—on March 10, 1997, on the new WB Network. It had a lot going for it, with strong, often sarcastic dialogue, believable teen characters, good alternative music that steered well clear of the "alternative mainstream," and plenty of action. Having a girl who was more than capable of kicking demonic butt helped a lot, too (even if Buffy only undertook the job reluctantly), showing a strong female character in a sympathetic light.

Buffy the Vampire Slayer didn't reach television screens completely unheralded. There'd been a 1992 movie of the same name, written by Joss Whedon, who was also the brains and main writing talent behind the series. But the Buffy of the movie was a much more straightforward proposition than the Buffy of the series. In a film that lasted less than two hours, there was little chance to really develop the characters and come to grips with any complexities they might have had. Nor was there the chance to examine the cultural and social quagmire known as high school, which Whedon would go on to look at with a painfully clear eye. On television, Buffy would become a fully-rounded character, as would those around her. There'd be doubts, hatreds, romances—and more than a bit of killing. Buffy herself represented the ultimate teenage outsider. She wanted to belong and be normal, but the fact that she was the chosen Slayer meant she could never quite fit into the regular mold. Think of it as a metaphor for most teenagers, put to a background of action.

By the same token, Angel, even in the earliest episodes, represented fantasy. He was the dark stranger who exuded both danger and romance—two big magnets. And the fact that he seemed to come from nowhere, and not be part of any scene (in other words, a man of mystery, as well as few words) only added to his allure. And the looks. . . . well, enough said about that.

It wasn't until the third episode that there was much contact between Angel and Buffy. Angel was certainly enough to threaten Xander, who had been developing a major crush on Buffy, and to make him realize he was out of his league here.

In that episode, for the first time Buffy was willing to let her guard down a little around Angel, and not treat him quite so warily. In fact, she went to the opposite extreme, becoming coy and flirtatious, although he never seemed to change at all. But he did give her a token of sorts—his leather jacket. Black, of course.

Notably, Buffy's feelings toward Angel, although full of fantasies, never descended into the idea of her being rescued by him. She was strong—she was the Slyer, after all—and someone who was more than capable of controlling her situations. She didn't need Angel in that way. It was about love, romance . . . and more than a smidgen of lust.

It wouldn't be until the season's sixth episode that people would be able to begin connecting the dots about David's character.

The story revealed Angel's deep secret—he was a vampire, and almost two hundred and fifty years old. But none of this could come out until he'd shown Buffy that her feelings toward him were reciprocated. Had she known before, of course, he'd have very likely found himself on the wrong end of a wooden stake.

As it turned out, the relationship between the two of them would be an exaggerated metaphor for any relationship, with its difficulties, incompatibilities, and ups and downs. That it wasn't going to be easy was immediately apparent with the appearance of

Darla, the vampire who'd made Angel into Angelus more than two centuries before.

The love between Buffy and Angel would be tested very quickly. Not only did she *want* to believe him, she trusted him—after all, she'd invited him into her home, something no Slayer would normally do to a vampire.

He certainly wasn't like other vampires, and as he told his story, it became apparent why. After joining the undead, he'd ravaged and murdered his way across his native Ireland, before moving on. He tortured, maimed, and murdered gleefully in England, before ending up in Hungary, where he'd feasted on a young gypsy girl.

The girl's Romany parents, on discovering their daughter's body, had set a curse on Angelus, as he was known. A vampire lived without a soul and without a conscience. The curse restored the conscience to Angel, and made him aware of, and repentant for, all the bad things he'd done, doomed to live in constant unhappiness. That was why, in his own way, he'd been helping Buffy. It was his way of atoning for all the evil he'd done in the past. And he began cutting his links with his own past, making even greater amends. It would make him a vampire who became a true outcast, even to other vampires.

Angel was a person of contradictions, and this helped explain a great deal about him, and the behavior he'd shown so far. It also set up many potential conflicts in the romance between Angel and Buffy. They loved each other, but love between a vampire and a Slayer could never run a straight, even path. They were both outsiders on the opposite extremes.

Anything between them would be disapproved of by everyone. He was a vampire and he was older, much more experienced; it was, in many ways, the ultimate Romeo and Juliet situation. Could love be enough to sustain them through all the problems they'd face? That question couldn't be answered here, but it set up a long development.

Angel's history would be enacted in flashback, but he'd truly come alive in the minds of millions of viewers, and turned from just another sidekick into a full-fledged heartthrob. To be sure, he was romanticized, albeit in a very dark way, but there was nothing wrong with that; where all the others had a strong streak of reality in them, grounded in the real world, Angel acted as the literally fantastic foil. It took a great deal to be able to pull that off, but David managed it with a rare style. The fact that the sparks between Angel and Buffy seemed completely natural only eased things along.

The audience had been given a great deal to consider, because Angel's past—and, indeed, his present—weren't simple. Nor was his relationship with Buffy anything less than complex. Giles, Buffy's Watcher, found something poetic in the very obvious love between Slayer and vampire—although he worried that it would end in heartbreak, one way or another, for Buffy, who was his responsibility.

Interestingly, at the end of the first season, the show hadn't yet been picked up for a second season by the WB network. Joss Whedon was confident that would happen, though, and in any event, he was right. *Buffy the Vampire Slayer* was a hit, albeit a cult one to begin with (and what constituted a hit on the new

WB network wasn't the same as what constituted a
hit on, say, ABC).

The characters had great appeal, and great depth,
which set them apart from so many television creations. They reflected, on a number of levels, the lives
of real teenagers, which was where their prime viewing audience lay. But they'd already moved beyond
that, to capture a much wider demographic, and become one of the breakout shows on the new network—much the way *Dawson's Creek* would be the
following season. Previously it had been Fox that had
seemed geared toward a younger audience; now the
WB had taken that mantle away from them.

For David, the first season had been great. Angel
was still a recurring character, but had become so
strong that he was, to all intents and purposes, a regular cast member. And with the renewal of the show
(something which had been pretty much a foregone
conclusion) that was exactly what he'd become.

His patience had paid off in a big way. He'd found
himself not only with a great character, but on one of
television's hottest shows, and along the way he'd become a true heartthrob. The scripts were uniformly
excellent, and the development of the characters and
their relationships meant there was plenty in store for
the future—particularly in the ongoing romance between Buffy and Angel.

The renewal lent him a sense of security. He was
doing the thing he'd dreamed of—making a living
from his acting. And that was more than merely scrap-
ing by; he was making a *good* living. He might have
taken the job, as he joked, to feed Bertha Blue, but
now he could keep her in the best gourmet dog food

on the market. He'd treated himself, buying a 1996 Ford Explorer, fitting in handily with the SUV culture that seemed to be everywhere—you were a nobody if you didn't have four-wheel drive. But that was the extent of his ostentation. Apart from that, he was exactly the same David he'd always been.

Prior to *Buffy* reaching the air, he was still doing live theater. In fact, even as rehearsals were underway, he found himself cast in an Equity waiver production of Sam Shephard's *Cowboy Mouth*, staged at the Hudson Theater in Hollywood, his highest-profile performance to date. But it was being part of the ensemble that made up the cast of *Buffy the Vampire Slayer* (or *BTVS*, as it's known to fans) that gave him the greatest satisfaction. Hoping they could all work together well had been a gamble, but one that had paid off handsomely.

In analyzing the way it had all worked out so well, David was quick to note that luck and chemistry had been factors. After all, the cast had been assembled individually, and the chemistry between them all had turned out to be very, very good. Obviously, it wasn't all sunshine every single minute, but a lot of that, he thought, could be attributed to the stress of working long, long hours, rather than any ego problems. People had times when they were more vulnerable or snappish, usually when they were exhausted, and everyone learned to make allowances for that. Overall, he'd been thrilled with the way the season had gone. Even if the cast had been picked as an ensemble, it couldn't have worked better.

Given the work he was doing it was just as well, he points out, that "I've always liked horror films. When I was a kid, *Frankenstein*, the original movie, scared the hell out of me. I've always been fascinated with the film *Nosferatu*, and when I saw the film the first time it was eerie. You have no choice but to get into the genre because you're surrounded by all these vampires and it's amazing when you have all these extras in vampire makeup, or you're in the graveyard shooting and you look around and see vampires hanging out, it's pretty wild. It's a lot of fun and it's a genre that Hollywood loves to portray."

Angel, of course, switched between his "human" face and his "vampire" face, which naturally required a lot of makeup. But, according to David, "the prosthetic part of it isn't too bad. Angel changes only when he's confronted by evil vampires, so he's usually showing up regular faced. But when he does change, it's usually not that bad of a process. It's pretty quick. The only painful part is taking it off. It's tedious because you can't just peel the stuff off because you'll rip your skin. So you have to easily take oil and use brushes to take it off." In fact, it took about an hour to apply the makeup, and a good forty minutes of work to remove it. When pressed, David will admit that "the pain comes in taking it off, it's tedious, very rough on your skin." Which may well explain why David has become a big fan of aloe vera gel. And for all those who wondered about Angel's tattoo, it's never been permanently fixed to David's body; in fact, it's tattoo ink, drawn on—and removed every day.

The hassle with makeup was a small price to pay for success, all things considered. And every actor wears makeup to a greater or lesser degree.

If there was one drawback to shooting a series, it was that the actors really had no idea what would be coming up in the weeks ahead. David could honestly say, "I have no idea. We get the scripts and it's very exciting to see what's going to happen with my character as it evolves. But, uh, I'm having a blast. It's a cool gig and, uh, the people are friendly and I'm fortunate to be there."

Obviously, Angel's main contact—in more ways than one—was with Buffy, and it was there that things had begun to sizzle.

"Most of my work has been with Sarah [Michelle Gellar], I see the other members of the cast but I haven't really had scenes with them. Working with Sarah is great." There was a definite chemistry between them that was waiting to be explored, but it only extended to the set. Beyond that they were friends, but there was never a hint of anything more. And that was only right. Sarah, who categorizes David as "a great dancer" (although maybe not as great as Xander, whose fans have given him his own dance website), is a professional, just like David. Business and romance could never mix among the cast of a weekly show; it would be asking for trouble.

More than that, David had become involved with someone. Aptly for a person playing a vampire born in Ireland, he'd met an Irish woman named Ingrid. She'd been born in Dublin, and worked in Los Angeles as a social worker. Beyond that, there was no information, and no pictures of the two of them together. But David had always been one for carefully separating his personal and private lives. He was a public figure now, a celebrity of sorts, but that didn't mean he couldn't have a truly private life as well. He didn't mind being photographed when he was out—after all, that also helped promote the show—but in

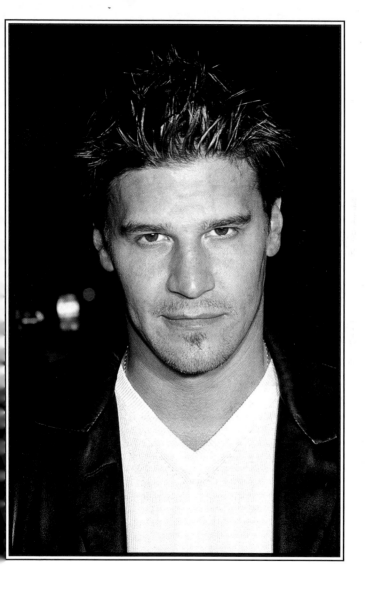

WITH SARAH MICHELLE GELLAR.
(©JOSEPH MARZULLO/RETNA LIMITED, USA)

WITH NICHOLAS BRENDON.
(©STEVE GRANITZ/RETNA LIMITED, USA)

his down time with his girlfriend, that was off limits.

Becoming a celebrity seemed strange at first, although he'd seen it happen with his father, and he'd learned from that. From an early age he'd been taught to respect his fans, and that was what he did. He might respond to a letter that particularly touched him, writing back to the fan—a letter, not e-mail.

That said, he has been known to follow up a letter to a fan with a phone call—which has certainly freaked out more than a few people.

When it's happened, it's invariably been a surprise to the fan, and at times they've thought the call was a joke—at least until David began referring to the letter, and which time they know it's for real, and David has really called them.

Maybe it was taking the personal touch a little too far, but it was the kind of gesture most celebrities would never think to make, and one that's set him apart. Maybe it's the Deadhead or the latent hippie in him that's made him that way, but basically he doesn't see himself as much different from the people who watch the show.

"It's a weird medium we're in," he observes. "The camera gets turned on you and you become famous—the same thing happens when you put cameras on lawyers, as we've seen."

Being an actor on a breakout show didn't make him any better than anyone else, simply more widely known. He might have been able to eat at the best restaurants Los Angeles had to offer, and probably even get the best tables in the house, but his sense of roots was so strong that rather than eating the cuisine of Le Dome, he'd sooner be at home with that Philly staple, the cheesesteak sandwich. Friends and family would send him care packages of them, lovingly prepared with the meat separate from the roll until David was ready to assemble it into the finished article and eat it.

And rather than being seen out and about, on the town all the time, he was happiest slipping away with Bertha Blue and Ingrid, getting away from L.A. on the weekends after five days of shooting. In the evenings he'd sit at home and read—when he had the chance. Any television series meant a lot of work, and very long days.

The majority of people work eight hours at a time, whether it's in school, an office, a store, wherever. It might be a shift, it might be a regular workday. But unless you're on overtime, it usually tops out at forty hours a week. Being on a television series is very different. The actor's day can run anywhere from ten to eighteen hours, depending how involved they are in the scenes being filmed that day. Multiply that by five days in a week, and you've got. . . . a lot of hours. And part of that means getting up early. A six o'clock call at the set is fairly common—which means that the actors have to be at the studio by then. In turn, that means they have to be up and showered a good hour before that, at five.

To be sure, they're driven to the studio and back home. They eat their meals at the studio. They're well paid, and stardom brings the opportunity to go on and make movies, where the money increases remarkably. But the majority of series get canceled, and the actors end up back in the audition line, doing minimum wage jobs, or drawing unemployment. It's a very lucky few who really make it big.

Every actor has spent time out of work—or "rest-ing" as they prefer to call it. So who's to blame them for taking advantage of every opportunity that comes. Sarah Michelle Gellar, for example, was using her summer break to film *I Know What You Did Last Summer* (and down the road there'd be *Scream 2*), which would prove to be a remarkably high-grossing film. Some of that audience might have been persuaded to tune into *Buffy*.

But Gellar had a much higher profile than David. She'd been acting since she was a child, and had enjoyed a good run, and a daytime Emmy, on the soap opera *All My Children* before moving on to *BTVS*. Other than playing Angel, no one had really ever heard of David Boreanaz. Granted, those who'd seen him all thought he was great—but so far those numbers weren't big enough to warrant the movie offers. He had yet to become a box office draw on his own account.

And that was fine with him. He could take the summer off and relax. After all, the last few months had been quite incredible, something or a roller coaster ride—although he was still waiting for the drop. It wasn't until the series was renewed by WB that he could truly breathe easily and begin really making plans for the future, and assessing what made the show resonate.

"The fact that it started out as a cult hit is brilliant," he analyzes. "I think that [the show] is appealing because it's an hour of fun—not-too-heavy thinking with a bit of humor and drama mixed in. It taps into people's adolescence and [they], in turn can identify with the characters. And it's done in a wild way."

And it kept him employed. Life was very, very good. Success, after years of nothing, was even better.

". . . I have a fear of failing," David explains. "This is a very hard business and as an actor you take on certain challenges and within that challenge you find yourself sometimes falling down.

"But within the falling down you learn more about yourself, so with the fear comes the time to realize who you are as a person and from that you learn from your mistakes, which makes you grow as a person."

CHAPTER FIVE

THE concept of a vampire with a conscience was certainly original, as was the idea of a cursed vampire. But the idea of the vampire as someone undead, who existed on the blood of living creatures, was far from new.

The vampire had existed in many mythologies, quite probably since before recorded history. The Romans had a word for them, as did the Greeks, although the main area of vampire belief seemed to be in the Balkan area of Europe—of course, the home of Count Dracula would be in Transylvania, located somewhere in Central Europe (actually, part of Romania).

For centuries, though, it remained part of mythology, in much the same way as centaurs, the creatures that were half-man, half-horse, or any number of other things that might have had some grounding in symbology, but which tended to stretch the mind as to their existence. Whereas the other creatures stayed in the mythological background, between 1600 and 1800 the idea of the vampire strode out of the storybooks and into real life. There were countless cases of supposed vampires. Not only did they occur in the Balkan region, but they spread west into the more "enlightened" areas of Europe. Even England and Ireland weren't immune from the tales and instances of vampire activity. By 1732, the word vampire had become a part of the English language. Corpses of suspected vampires were exhumed, and put to final rest with a stake through their hearts.

For most people, however, the idea of the vampire didn't become anything more than superstition until the publication, in 1897, of Bram Stoker's novel, *Dracula*. Dracula himself was based on the rather gruesome character of Vlad the Impaler (actually Vlad III Dracula), who ruled Wallachia three times, first in 1448, then again in 1456, and finally 1476. The real Dracula wasn't a vampire, but his nickname of "the Impaler" was certainly justified—he would impale thousands at a time, not only his enemies, but also his own subjects.

It was Stoker who truly crystalized the vampire myth into something tangible, who codified it. A vampire needed earth from his native land in order to rest. A crucifix—the main symbol of Christianity—became a powerful weapon against vampires, as did holy water. For the first times, the potency of garlic as a weapon to ward off vampires was revealed in Stoker's book.

A wooden stake was the only thing that could kill a vampire. In particular, ash and juniper were powerful—and the stake had to go through the vampire's heart. Anywhere else was just a wound.

While people nowadays take for granted the idea that sunlight destroys vampires, that was not part of Stoker's lore. His vampires could be outside during the day without fear—although it did make them much weaker.

And while tales of vampires invading people's houses to feast on their blood were widespread, the lore was that a vampire couldn't enter a house unless first invited—although the vampire would use all manner of tricks to get an invitation. Vampires cast no shadow. A vampire could not see himself in the mirror; because he wasn't a real person, there was no reflection (although in Rudyard Kipling's story, "The Vampire," which was published the same year as *Dracula*, vampires *could* see their reflections).

In the realms of literature, that was the way things stayed, more or less, until Anne Rice began writing about vampires. She completely revised the idea of the vampire, giving them depth, personality, and a great deal more appeal. Indeed, the modern popularity of vampire mythology (which extends as far as people having their incisors sharpened to resemble fangs) is because of Rice's work in her books that comprise *The Vampire Chronicles*.

Whereas the vampires of myth and literature had previously seemed terrifying beings, interested only in blood, Rice's creations were sensual and sexy. Lestat himself had charm and warmth. He was seductive. And he, like other vampires, wasn't susceptible to the power of garlic, and only fire—not a wooden stake—could kill him and his kind. If a vampire were old enough, sunlight couldn't kill him.

But one vampire constant that Rice adhered to was the fact that vampires couldn't age. They remained whatever age they were when "sired."

It was film and television, far more than books, that kept the idea of vampires alive in people's minds. There was the chilling silent classic from Germany,

Nosferatu, which adapted *Dracula* (without using the name) in a way that's rarely been equaled since. Its atmosphere went beyond ghostly, all the way to terrifying. It was followed by another silent film, *The Case of the Sussex Vampire*, a supposed Sherlock Holmes mystery. But really, it was with the advent of the talkies that the vampire took flight, most especially in 1931's *Dracula*, with Bela Lugosi in the title role—the one with which his name remains associated.

From there, films about vampires went in and out of style, although they tended toward the low-budget and campy, to just out-and-out bloodthirsty horror. The image of the vampire had been established; it didn't need to be built upon. And there were, of course, comedies about vampires, ranging from *Love at First Bite* (1979) to the bizarre *To Have and Have Not: A Vampire in McDonald's* (1977).

It wasn't until the nineties that the movies examined vampires in greater depth. *Bram Stoker's Dracula*, directed by Francis Ford Coppola in 1992, wasn't the biggest commercial or critical success, but it did go beneath the surface of the story to flesh out many of the story's more psychological elements. Stoker's novel, written during the repressive Victorian age, had the vampire as something of a romantic outsider, one who defied convention—and there was an unwritten sexual subtext about it all. It was lush, very romantic—all Dracula really wanted was the woman who was the image of his late wife—and very sexy. The note of Victorian repression came in the person of Dr. Van Helsing, the straightforward and methodical vampire killer.

Interview with a Vampire, the screen version of

Anne Rice's famous book, was much more overtly sensual, helped along by stars Tom Cruise and Brad Pitt in the main roles. It was erotic and dangerous without ever being explicit—tapping very well into the images created in Rice's writing. Her vampires could be as much about thought and reflection as about action—and sex could be much more than a deep kiss on the neck.

All in all, around one hundred films have been devoted to vampires—including, of course, the original *Buffy the Vampire Slayer*, whose idea, by Joss Whedon, was much better than its execution.

Vampires have also been featured on television long before Buffy staked her first victim in Sunnydale. On *The Munsters,* both Grandpa and Lily were vampires, albeit of the comedic kind. But, pre-*Buffy*, the vampire cult hit of the small screen was undoubtedly *Dark Shadows*, the soap opera than ran on ABC from 1966 to 1971, and which has since cropped up on reruns and video. Starring a two-hundred-year-old vampire named Barnabas Collins, played by Jonathan Frid, it was certainly the most unusual daytime soap ever to grace the airwaves.

The Night Stalker, from the 1970s, was quite horrific for a little while, but the writers seemed to quickly run out of story lines. For a good fifteen years after that, vampires were notable by their absence from television.

Just as it did in the movies, the nineties seemed to bring a new vampire sensibility to the small screen. In both *Forever Knight* and *Kindred: The Embraced*, the vampires were more than blood sucking horrors. They also possessed sensitive sides. Indeed, watch any series, and you can almost see the seeds of Angel.

The lead of *Forever Knight* was an ancient vampire working as a homicide detective, his attempt to make good all the evil he'd done in the past. In *Kindred: The Embraced*, the ruler of San Francisco's vampire clans had to enforce the "vampire laws," which precluded taking human lives or turning humans into vampires against their will (he would obviously have been working overtime in Sunnydale).

While all of these succeeded or failed in their own ways, they laid a strong groundwork for the television *Buffy*.

It would be, thankfully, a long way from the movie of *Buffy* that had come from Joss Whedon's pen. His script was optioned in 1988, but the film itself didn't appear until 1992. Whedon wanted to show someone taking charge of their own life, but also to poke a little fun at the horror genre—"So I decided to make a movie where a blonde girl walks into a dark room and kicks butt instead." With Kristy Swanson in the title role, and Luke Perry (fresh from *Beverly Hills 90210*) as her romantic interest, with Donald Sutherland as the Watcher, alongside Rutger Hauer and Pee Wee Herman in evil roles, it should have done very well.

There's a vast distance between should and did, however. Fox expected teens to be lining up, if only for Luke Perry, and spent a lot of money promoting the movie—all to no avail. If anything, the film proved more popular with adults. Even then, it didn't exactly set the box office on fire, grossing just over $16 million in the U.S.

One thing greatly lacking in the film was any real sense of menace. The movie Buffy was a machine, or perhaps a Valley girl type with martial arts skills.

There was little depth to her, and no complexity. And that wasn't quite Whedon's original intention.

"In the movie, the director took an action/horror/comedy script and went only with the comedy," he says. But he never expected to get a chance to right the balance, until, out of the blue, Gail Berman of Sandollar Productions (which had optioned the screenplay in 1988) approached him. He was interested—but he wanted creative control, to come up with a show that would be like *My So-Called Life* meeting *The X-Files*.

Fox television turned it down, but the upstart WB was eager, especially after seeing Whedon's twenty-four minute "presentation." It was essentially a show reel that Whedon had written, directed, and, according to some rumors, even financed. The basic cast and characters were in place (although Riff Regan, and not Alyson Hannigan, played Willow), with the exception of Angel. And Sarah Michelle Gellar didn't have Buffy's famous blonde locks yet, either. Still, it gave a taste of what was to come, although in the very rough, early stages.

The WB was convinced, according to Susanne Daniels, executive vice president of programming: "As soon as we saw his pilot script, we knew we had something unique, but it wasn't until the casting process, when we met Sarah, that we knew we had our first potential breakthrough show. *Buffy* is really scary, it's really sexy, and it's really funny. We think it's a show that has it all."

The network wasn't too keen on the title, however; some felt it was simply far too eighties. But Whedon prevailed, although it was notable that by the second season, the words *"the Vampire slayer"* had been made a lot smaller.

Angel was really the final piece of the puzzle, the last-minute addition who really provided the link between the Slayerettes (aka the Scooby Gang) and the Underworld. While part of neither, he was able to move between the two. According to the "back story" (which filled in his history), after being cursed, Angel had drifted, more or less a nonperson, full of remorse at everything he'd done. He'd come to America, and had been living as a homeless person when he was discovered by the demon Whistler in New York, early in the nineties. Whistler was the one who forced him back onto his feet, and gave him a push in the right direction.

Somehow Angel knew who the Slayer was, and where she lived. He traveled to California, in fact to Los Angeles, where he observed Buffy in action without ever contacting her. Then, when she and her mother packed and made a fresh start in Sunnydale, Angel was there, and suddenly made his presence known.

He was the romantic character the series needed, darker and more experienced in the ways of the world than the others, one who'd not only seen evil but also committed it. His redemption through the curse gave him greater depth, and a lingering, reflective sorrow—the brooding quality so many fans love in Angel. That he had his personal demons—the kind that could be easily destroyed—was obvious in the first season. But really, it was only in the episode "Angel" that people came to understand the things that plagued him. And the fact of the matter was that no matter how much good he did, how much he helped the Slayer keep the world safe, it could never atone for all the evil he'd done in the past. And Angel knew it. So he was trapped.

More than trapped, really. He was in an impossible situation, because he was a vampire in love with a Slayer, a situation that could bring no one a happy ending.

Playing a character of mystery and depth was a challenge, from episode to episode. But it was a challenge that David savored. He'd found a focus, then every day he'd arrive on the set, ready to work, fully prepared for the day's shooting, but still loose enough to let things happen, if that was the way it went. In many ways, those moments when things took off unexpectedly were the most exciting for him, and when he felt the most a part of angel. But those are the moments any actor lives for. When something seems to go wrong, but on playback it turns out to be something different. David loved that.

In particular, he was pleased by the scenes he'd shared with Gellar.

They'd obviously worked together a lot during the first season, and the chemistry between them was quite remarkable and believable. They'd quickly managed to grasp each other's styles and abilities and work with them, which made the job a real delight for David. Quite often, he was able to complete a scene with her and know in his bones that it was really good. At the same time, there had been occasions where he'd thought things hadn't worked, only to realize later that it had been fine. But even the real mistakes, the ones that *didn't* work, gave him a chance to learn—and that was as important as success.

He remained very wary of his new-found fame, however.

He was, in fact, very wary of the word and all that went with it. If anything, he still wanted to keep fame at a distance, to remain a regular kind of guy, which was how he saw himself, and how he was most comfortable. But as the show's popularity grew, that became harder and harder to do. David did try and keep it all in check, though, to remain very much in touch with his roots, aware of where he came from.

Celebrity did have an upside, though. "You do get little perks," David points out, "free stuff in the mail, or a nice pair of Nike shoes, which was nice. Those things come with the territory. Sometimes now I'm able to get a table more quickly at a restaurant—and I can buy my dogs more food."

The summer break, for him, offered a chance to put everything into perspective. Since he'd been hired there'd been barely chance to catch his breath, let alone do the things he truly loved—or even sleep a full night, for that matter. He needed a chance to come down and take his bearings. Yes, life was great, and he had at least another full season of work to look forward to. He was making a good living as an actor—but he didn't want to lose track of himself in the process.

For a start, time off gave him the opportunity to concentrate on his relationship with Ingrid. The hours he'd worked, and the intensity he had to keep up for his role, meant that during the shooting season he was inevitably a little distracted. Now he could devote time to her, and the things they could do together. He could roam all over with Bertha Blue (and the com-

panion he'd picked up for her, a Chinese Crested),
who'd seen a lot less of him lately.

He did bring Bertha Blue to the set sometimes, but
it wasn't easy. When David was working, she had to
be locked up in his trailer, which wasn't the perfect
solution. However, she couldn't be allowed to run
loose, obviously. Still, it was a pleasure to finish a
scene, go into his trailer and have her waiting eagerly
for him.

The big question was what Joss Whedon and his
scriptwriters would do with Angel during the show's
second season. There were a multitude of possibilities,
the most obvious of which was to develop his relationship with Buffy. That they loved each other had
already been established—but what could you do with
a romance between a vampire and a Slayer? It was
one of the great forbidden loves, a real Romeo and
Juliet situation—with a guaranteed tragic end. Angel,
of course, had more than two hundred years on
Buffy—girls do date older men, but that was probably
going a bit far—and he'd seen and done things she
couldn't imagine, and probably wouldn't want to.
He'd told her of his dark past, but in reality, she had
no conception of quite how evil he could be. She was
young, just about to enter her junior year, and however worldly her Slayer activities had made her, she
was still naive.

During the short first season of the show, Angel's
role had expanded from observer and informant to
participant in the fight against evil at the Hellmouth.
The second season would give him a chance to do
even more, David supposed—maybe fight alongside
Buffy. If he didn't become an active member of the

Scooby Gang, he could be the outsider with special knowledge who could help.

For now, though, that would remain shrouded in mystery. The writers weren't telling the actors anything. They'd find out when they reported back to work after the summer break. So David filled his time with relaxing activities, with biking and hiking, and some time on the golf course.

For someone who'd played football and school, and who loved basketball, it might have seemed a tame sport. But David had played a little in college, and after he'd settled in California, he'd become hooked on it. Perhaps it was just as well. Games like basketball and hockey had been ruled out by the doctor because of his knee problems. So it gave him exercise, and some sort of competition. More than that, he found it could relax his mind, take his thoughts away from whatever worries he had and leave him refreshed. And around Los Angeles, there was rarely the problem of being rained out.

So David spent the summer of '97 enjoying himself, kicking back—but with a feeling of security behind him. He'd waited, and in true karmic fashion, the good things had come to him. After trusting was fulfillment; it all felt right.

CHAPTER SIX

DAVID
was more than ready for work to begin after the break.
All the cast were. In a sense it was like coming home
to family after some time away. But people on a new
show tend to bond that way; it's them against the
world, and they do stick together.

"We're very close. Sometimes we go to a movie
or go get a drink," David says. And given the way
the cast had to work together like a family, that was
probably all for the best.

One thing none of the actors knew was whether
there'd be any major changes going into the second
season. It was always possible that another major
character might be added, something along those
lines. But Whedon, who retained creative control,
knew he'd achieved the balance in numbers and tem-
peraments that he needed for the show. It was working fine, so why mess with it?

At the same time, it couldn't just be Buffy battling
the monster of the week. That would get old very
quickly. Things had to develop. There would be story
arcs—each episode standing alone, but connected to
others. And the characters would grow, their relationships, both with each other and with others, would

change. That wasn't just the way of high schoolers, it was the way of everyone.

For David, it promised to be a bust season. During the first series, Angel had been more or less a guest character, although an important one. Now he'd become part of the regular cast, which meant, obviously, that he was going to become more important and involved in the story lines.

And where could the romance between Buffy and Angel go?

Initially, in the premier episode, it seemed like they could go nowhere.

It seemed as if Angel was still on the periphery, but that was about to change, as his past came back to haunt him. While it had been downplayed to a great extent, there had been more than a few hints about Angel's history, and some specifics. He'd killed gleefully, and sired more than his share of vampires, including Drusilla and Spike.

Apart from being vampires, Spike and Drusilla also offer the show's Goth content—which was fair enough. The whole Goth subculture still exists in high school, and who better to represent it than a pair of vampires, really, some true Bat Cavers, as it were.

In fact, although they sounded it, neither Marsters nor Landau was English, but adopted the accents to offer some history and sense of foreignness to the characters—and won the approval of the real resident Brit, Anthony Head.

"The first week that I was shooting..... ." Marsters recalls, "I asked him how my accent was, because his is very similar to the one I'm trying to get, and he said, 'Well, it's very good; you just can't tell where you're from.' And, by the way, Anthony isn't using his real accent for the show. In real life, he sounds more like Spike hopefully does."

To have two vampires so obviously in love was something new, but of course Whedon wanted to give it a bit of a twist

"Joss's initial concept was that we were to be the 'Sid'N'Nancy' of the Sunnydale vampire set," Landau explains. "At first, James was doing it in a Southern U.S. accent, but then he did a complete turnaround and became Spike."

"Joss Whedon really wanted a Sid Vicious sort of thing," Marsters continues. "They thought that my character should have a dramatic look. They tried [my hair] black and it didn't quite look what they wanted, so they decided to go exactly the opposite way. In the beginning Billy Idol wasn't really in the mix. But I have to be really careful not to sneer like him!"

The codependent relationship between Spike and Drusilla offered an interesting contrast to the relationship between Angel and Buffy, where Angel seemed, at least on the surface, so reticent.

The truth was that Angel was scared of losing emotional control. As a vampire he'd had no real control, and had desired none. Now, reformed, that tight control was what kept him apart—from everything. Distance was his friend. Did he know everything the curse entailed, and was that why he couldn't really let himself admit he was as much in love with Buffy as she was with him? Whatever the real reason, he was scared to give in to his feelings. There did seem to be some future for them, since they at least made a semi-date, to go out for coffee.

Eventually, of course, Angel had to come to terms

with the fact that Buffy was his true soulmate, that they were two sides of the same coin.

Like any mirror of real life, no relationship on television could progress smoothly. For a start, there'd be little drama to it, and second, the characters would never grow. So having moved to a new level, it was time for Buffy and Angel to experience a few conflicts. It was only fitting that they should all come from the past—where most of our demons really seem to dwell.

It was interesting that, as the writers showed more of Angel, and his role in the series expanded, he was being shown in two ways—as the vampire with very human traits and a taste for goodness, but also as someone with a despicable past. Yes, it gave him depth, but showing the evil streak ran the risk of alienating some viewers from the character. It was a fine line to walk, but at least showing his bad deeds to be in the past gave real hope for Angel in the present and the future.

Gradually, the producers had brought a lot of focus on the character of Angel. From something of a shadowy figure, he'd been given three full dimensions, and was one of the mainstays of the cast. But he'd proved to be one of the real hits of the first season, so that wasn't too surprising. And the depth was necessary for him to truly work as a character, since his romance with Buffy was continuing to grow. At the same time, the writers couldn't give him a disproportionate amount of airtime.

One issue the show had yet to do more than barely touch on was sex. While it had been discussed, and there had been roundabout references and innuendoes, it had rarely been confronted. But the majority of the characters were in high school, and sexual discovery would be, for many of them, part of the experience of growing. The audience did know that Buffy was a virgin; that much had been established. But would they move her past that in her relationship with Angel, or would things just be allowed to lie?

What Buffy didn't know was the content of the curse on Angel. If he enjoyed even one minute's perfect happiness, he'd revert to being a real vampire. And when Angel made love to Buffy his happiness lingered much longer than a minute . . .

But it had the effect of lifting the curse and Angel backslid into Angelus.

The new Angel (or, really, the old Angelus) offered David a lot of opportunities as an actor.

"When Angel's evil, he has no sense of anything," David says. "His soul is really torn up, and offering the blacker side of Angel was a lot of fun. It was easy for me, in a sense, because the writing was so pure and simple, it gave me an opportunity to expand personality traits and get into his head. And with each episode I learned more, whether it be twisting a flower in a kind of weird way while I was talking to a girl or something that was way out there." He points out that, "with Angel's good side, I wasn't really exploring as much, as far as his being as outgoing as I wanted to be."

But the evil that would be Angelus was only just beginning. If he seemed bad now, there would be much worse to come. Emotionally, it had destroyed Buffy. She was strong on the outside, as a Slayer, where it was a direct battle of good and evil. That required no thought, only action, and her young age and quick reactions were a plus. Having to deal with love and loss was a different matter. There it was obvious that she hadn't grown up yet, and that she had to cope with losing the first real love of her life. Not just losing him as if he'd died, but having him turn against her, and knowing that she was, at least in part, responsible.

It was the turning point of the entire season. And it was completely unexpected, which made it all the more dramatic. For now, at least, Angel had plenty to sink his teeth into, literally and metaphorically. By setting up a friend and lover as an enemy, the writers had created a very interesting dynamic in the show. Everyone thought they knew Angel, and they'd come to trust him, albeit hesitantly. Now they all—especially Buffy—had to realize they didn't know him at all, that the person they'd liked and loved had been completely swept away.

More than anyone, Buffy was in an impossible situation. She couldn't forget her love for Angel. But she was also the Slayer, whose function was to rid the world of vampires. And that meant she had to kill the person she still loved—even if he wasn't that person any more. It was a situation no teenager should have been in, but it was happening.

For David, it promised a strong second half of the season. But it did raise the question of how viewers would react to the evil Angel. The brooding, tormented character had won a lot of fans, and pictures of David had ended up on a lot of lockers and bedroom walls. Would people be turned off by this turn of events? Or would they all be rooting for the good Angel to win through in the end (always assuming that was even possible)? Having set up the situation, the writers had opened the way for any number of ongoing story lines—including a possible renewal of a relationship between Angel and Drusilla.

Even the actors didn't yet know where it would all go, and that was for the best. There was no way they could second-guess the writers, or inadvertently give away clues as to the development of the story. But big trouble was coming to Sunnydale. That much was beyond any kind of dispute.

CHAPTER SEVEN

HOW did people react to the huge change in Angel? Well, it was mixed. David and the other actors loved it. Viewers, however, didn't always take the same tone.

"It made people angry," creator Joss Whedon admits. "It was the only thing I could have done really, in a way."

But as Anthony Head points out, "They got over it, didn't they? It makes for wonderful tension between us all. It's great storytelling—that's what Joss is brilliant at. The romance could only go so far and then it becomes like a daytime soap. Basically, seeing Angel stalk Buffy, it means nothing unless there are real stakes."

"A lot of [fans] preferred the evil Angel and a lot of them didn't," David says. "I liked it; anytime you can change up and play something different, that's great. It was challenging. I remember being very scared. But if I'm not afraid of something, why do it?"

Still, it definitely wasn't always easy.

"On the set, it was particularly hard doing scenes with Sarah, because she didn't see Angel as an evil type, and all of a sudden there he was," recalls David.

"For the most part, the relationship between Buffy and Angel had almost been a *Beauty and the Beast* type of thing. Buffy knew what angel was, but she still loved him. Then the transition came, and it was hard for her, and also for me, to adjust. To help Sarah with that transition, after each scene I made it a point to confirm to her that, 'I'm here for you, I'm not here against you. This is not who I am.' I believe there has to be a coming-down period where you hug the other actor, or help the other person, and even help yourself get out of the turmoil that's been created, instead of being submerged in it. As harrowing as that can be sometimes, it's part of the acting process, and one I would never even think of giving up."

And Gellar agrees that it wasn't easy.

"There were times we'd have it out for the camera and then he'd have to come and hold me until I stopped crying and remembered that this is David, not the devil!"

In large part, that was because of the friendship that had grown between David and Sarah.

"The scariest thing we've done is when Angel went bad," she admitted at the time. "David and I have become very close over the two-and-a-half years we've known each other, and we have this purely platonic love for each other that made it very hard after his character went bad and did horrible things."

He certainly wouldn't have to think of giving up anything soon, since Angel was going to be a part of every episode, at least for the rest of the season, the constant thorn in Buffy's side, until, at the climax, she dispatched him to hell.

There was, of course, a very Christian irony in sending a cursed Angel to hell. He'd sinned, and sinned very grievously, and those sins had to be paid for. Hell, or purgatory, or wherever, was the place for that within the Christian religion.

It was, however, the only course the writers could take. For Angel to have been cursed, to suddenly have him restored and brooding, would not have been enough. He'd have been like the criminal who apologized and assumed everything would then be fine. There had to be atonement, a payback—and hell was far worse than any jail cell. Like anyone who'd done wrong, angel had to be seen to pay for his crimes.

It was the first time a full regular cast member had gone out of the series. But had Angel truly gone? He'd been sent to hell; he hadn't been killed. The way was open, at least in theory, for him to return. How and when might have been undecided, but it seemed likely, if only because of the popularity of both David and his character, that he would be back in the third season.

What cemented that was the news, just after the season had closed, that Angel would have his own spinoff series in the 1999–2000 season. Now, it was impossible for them to just leave him for a year, then bring him back in his own show. It wouldn't have washed. People would have forgotten who Angel was, and others would have simply stopped caring. So that meant, beyond a shadow of a doubt, that Angel would be back in season three. Which was great news for all those who'd swooned over him in the past.

It did set up plenty of intriguing possibilities, however. How would he return? What would he be like now? And what, if anything, could happen between him and Buffy?

The second season of *Buffy the Vampire Slayer* had

seen it grow from cult item to television success story. It still wasn't going to be cracking the twenty most-watched shows, but it had developed a strong audience, once that extended far beyond teenagers. The writing crackled, the characters had depth and resonance. It could turn from funny to deadly serious on a dime. It was perfectly fair to say there was no other show like it on TV.

And it had developed its own icons in Sarah Michelle Gellar and David Boreanaz. They might be doomed as lovers, but as heartthrobs they had it all going on. In the middle of 1999, *FHM* magazine would name Sarah as *the* sexiest woman, topping a list of one hundred. But that was only telling people what a lot of them had already realized a year before. She was a babe.

David had been the breakout, though. While the good Angel and the evil Angelus both had their adherents, there was no doubt that David himself had won a lot of female fans. There was an edge of danger to him, and that was remarkably alluring—it was something that had always attracted some women, and always would. If he returned, having paid for all his bad work, then he'd be cleansed, absolved, and able to start afresh in the minds of the fans. That was definitely something the writers would be considering. While the memories of evil would linger, he be untainted, like a baby, in a way, although gripped by the knowledge of all he'd done—for which he'd suffer eternally.

The writers had taken a lot of chances during the second season, both with the romance between Buffy and Angel, and especially with the character of Angel himself. But they'd all paid off remarkably well, and resulted in stories that were powerful. Fantastic at times, but always with a grounding that spoke, at least indirectly, to teens.

The year had been grueling, and had taken its toll, physically and emotionally, on everyone involved with the show. The first season had been short; this had been full-length, and they were all more than ready for a break.

CHAPTER EIGHT

THE cast and producers might have dreamed that *Buffy* would become huge, but probably none of them had seriously expected the major cult hit it ended up becoming—not only in the U.S., but around the world. Britain had also taken to the show, along with several other countries. And that meant more celebrity for the actors.

That translated into film offers and television appearances. David had been a guest on *The Rosie O'Donnell Show* on April 20, 1998, and then, on May 2, he was the guest star on *MadTV*, where he took part in a skit, playing himself. A couple of years ago, none of this could have happened; David was just another hopeful in a city full of hopefuls. But time, and a hit show, changed everything. And now the film offers were coming in. Sarah Michelle Gellar had cultivated a film career, Alyson Hannigan and Seth Green had both made movies. What would David do?

The simple answer was . . . nothing. He took the summer off, as befitted the laid-back lifestyle he preferred. Well, why not? He'd worked hard for nine months, long hours every day. But beyond the grueling physical schedule, there was also the emotional toll of playing Angel. It was draining, because, like any good actor, he put a lot of himself into the character. He needed to get away.

"This last summer I had a chance to do a movie role," he would recall later, "but then a friend of mine suggested I take a trip to Africa, which, on the spur of the moment, I decided to do. I had one of the most spiritual experiences of my life there. Anybody who wants to fight his fears, see the real self, peel all those layers away, be as vulnerable as you can, should go on a trip like that."

Going through that was another way to get to the place David calls "The Zone," where everything else simply drops away, and you become at peace, at one with everything. It might sound somewhat like hippie philosophy, or something New Age, but David does have those sides to him. He's a person who will gladly read self-help books (his father introduced him to the work of Og Mandino when he was young, and David has all his books, to which he often returns for inspiration and reinforcement).

Someone who makes his living playing a vampire might seem an unlikely candidate to be a New Age man, but like most people, David is a mass of contradictions. You might not expect a former jock to be so sensitive, but he is. There are facets to him that he doesn't always need to show.

And now he had his own show to look forward to. Granted, it was still a full year away (and a lot could happen in television in a year), but the promise of it was gratifying—it made all the reverses he'd suffered in the past worthwhile. He'd done some astonishing work in the season that had just finished, and it augured well for the future. For the moment he had something that all actors crave, but few find—security.

In his personal life, too, there was security, as he and Ingrid married. It was a quiet, private ceremony that didn't make the tabloids—in fact, it hardly made the news at all. Just family and friends attended, and the only photographs were those taken for the wedding album. And it was particularly fitting, given Ingrid's Irish background, and the symbolism for Angel, that they used a claddagh ring as their wedding band.

It was a time for relaxing, for letting life happen, rather than trying to kick-start anything. He was patient enough to let things develop in their own time, as he'd already shown. And he was still young, with many years still ahead of him in the business. What he wanted, more than anything, was to enjoy himself, not to be stressed out going from one project to the next and constantly running on a deadline. That was a good way to exhaust yourself, and not always be able to give your best. It was important to keep a perspective, to be able to kick back, look at things, laugh, and have the leisure to savor the occasional margarita.

Even more worrying was the danger of taking a job just for the sake of doing a job. The offers were there, but he was concerned about overexposing himself, and taking work just to keep his profile high. It was much more important to David that the work he did be good, that he find roles to be passionate about, that he wouldn't be ashamed of in a few years.

It was a good point. The list of actors who'd tried to do too much, too soon was a long casualty list. It showed that David had a wise head on his shoulders, being more cautious about things. And, although he was now considered famous, in his view, nothing much had altered. He was still the same person he'd always been, and he refused to believe that things had to change that much. He couldn't look in the mirror and see a star—all he saw was the same face that had looked back at him every morning of his life. If there was any satisfaction, it was in doing good work on a great show.

That didn't mean he just went in, did his stuff, and gave it no more thought. Quite the opposite. He'd spent a great deal of time considering Angel, who was not only his bread and butter, but also his future.

"I'd like Angel to be able to go to Las Vegas on road trips, spend the night with my vampire friends," he says. "You don't want to take your work home and think about the show, but you do inevitably because you are part of it and it is part of you. There is a lot to him that I would like to explore. He's got a good side, and he's got a bad side. How you keep that balanced is pretty interesting. Sure, he can mope around and be sad and brooding, or he can try to make a difference, somehow, in somebody's life. . . . Sure you make your amends and go on with it."

In his own life, David was trying to make a difference. While he wasn't one to generally become involved in promoting products, he had agreed to lend his name to the Levi's Original Spin Program. He got to design his own jeans, and, later in the fall, would tour with the program, appearing in Boston, Chicago, Dallas, and San Diego during November, signing autographs.

"The reason I was attracted to this is because the benefits are going to an organization called Peace 2000 . . . they create 'peace zones' in cities. [And] these kids paint these unbelievable murals. They're really cool." Apart from personal appearances, his involvement would be in designing jeans, which would be used to raise money for the cause.

"Celebrity jeans designed by Snoop Doggy Dogg, Tyra Banks and myself will be auctioned off and the proceeds will go to the organization."

David's particular style of Levi's, as custom made for him, were classic fit, with a boot cut leg, button fly, in black stonewash.

That aside, he spent the summer kicking back, both looking ahead and looking back. His next two years were already planned out, which was a wonderful feeling. There'd be no more parking cars or handing out towels for him now. He was established, a television name, but one who'd shown his prowess as an actor more than as a face. He understood full well the danger of being admired for his looks rather than his talent. It tended to make for a very brief career, and that was one thing he didn't want.

He'd become an actor because that was what he loved, not because he had visions of his face plastered on posters; the fact that had happened was pure luck and circumstance. He wanted challenge and longevity, work where he could make people believe in his character, where they saw not him, but the person he was playing.

While the success of Angel, and the prospect of his own show, were both tantalizing, they did somehow deflect from the real purpose. Yes, it was great to know that he was going to be a star. Yes, it was lovely to have fans. But he hadn't particularly sought fame, just a living, and everything else came as a bonus—albeit a massive one.

He still had goals—to do the very best work he could, and eventually to direct. After all, he had a degree in film, and that was what most film graduates did. He now understood things from both sides of the camera, and he'd learned a great deal, with a lot of practical experience. When the chance eventually came for him to direct something, whether it was in television, on the stage, or a film, he'd be able to bring that experience to bear.

One thing about having a name; it opened doors. There was a good chance that, at some point in the not too distant future, David *would* be able to direct, when he felt ready. Fame would help his career, as long as he used it wisely, and wasn't carried away by it. But that, from all his reactions, seemed unlikely. His feet were firmly planted on the ground, and being married to someone who wasn't involved in the business meant that he also had a life away from entertainment. It offered him balance in a world that was too often completely unbalanced, and lent him perspective. Ingrid was a social worker, dealing with very real problems, urgent problems of life and death that people had to face, not questions of who got the biggest trailer on a lot or something equally trivial.

But his summer of freedom would soon come to an end, and it would be back to the set. Once again, like the rest of the cast, he knew next to nothing about the writers' plans for the season.

"I don't know much about this season and Joss's plans, they don't tell me much until we get closer." Nor did he know that much about his own show: "It's Joss's idea, Joss's baby, what I do know I'm sworn to secrecy about."

Like any show, *Buffy the Vampire Slayer* had gathered some very serious fans, and like most shows that came under the fantasy/science fiction umbrella, a lot of them got together at conventions. The cast of *Buffy*, along with Joss Whedon, attended one, the San Diego Comic Book Convention, which proved to be something of an eye-opener. The people who came to meet them were quite hardcore about the show, people who'd memorized dialogue, who knew even the most trivial details—often more than the cast themselves ("Those are some serious fans," David notes). It was, notably, the first time that the cast had really met the people who made the show a success—the fans.

"It's been really great," David says of the experience. "The response has been overwhelming."

David has always been one to take a personal interest in his fan mail; he'd been known to reply, by hand, to some letters, and even to make phone calls. But his involvement also hit the Web, from time to time. No technophobe, David knew how to use a computer, and wasn't shy about it. From time to time he'd visit some of the *Buffy* Web sites—whose number seemed to grow every day, most of them, of course, unofficial. It let him know what people thought of the show and the characters, and he wasn't averse to leaving his own comments, or even taking part in some online chat, where that was possible. This was the 1990s, and this was how people communicated—so why shouldn't he be a part of it. Whatever he wrote was seen by thousands of fans. His message reached a large number of people very quickly, and there was absolutely nothing wrong with that.

In terms of weather and season, summer was far

from over when David returned to work (if summer could ever be said to leave Southern California). But he was rested and fit, and ready to return. Angel had a lot to do. . . .

CHAPTER NINE

THE question was *how* could Angel return? Granted, this was television, and fantasy, where anything was possible, but getting people out of hell had never been an easy task—even for a Slayer or a Watcher.

However, return he did, without explanation, although it seemed implicit that the love of a good woman had dedeemed him

Of course, it all raised questions, some of which would be answered in due course. Certainly, the reappearance of Angel put Buffy in an emotional quandary. Just as she believed she had been able to put him behind her, there he was again. But instead of being his old, strong self, there was a weakness and vulnerability about him—perhaps not too surprising after a century of being tortured in hell. He *needed* Buffy, and she was still in love with him.

But a realization came to Buffy. She couldn't be with Angel any more, and told him so. It was for the safety of her heart.

But could her resolution last?

Of course not; that would have been too easy. But Buffy had come to the realization that, whatever she felt, to an extent she and Angel were fooling themselves. The love was real, the fact that they really dared be together was not.

And what of Angel and Buffy . . . what could the future hold for them? Not a great deal, seemed to be the answer. They could love each other, but could never be lovers again. The only answer, at least in the short term, was to remain friends and keep the relationship part of things on hold. And over the next couple of episodes they realized, in the best possible way, that any kind of future together was impossible. It was a love that just refused to work out, which was why Angel told Buffy he was going to be leaving.

But it *was* love, that much was beyond doubt, which would be proved as the season moved toward the inevitable big finale. A couple of days after the first part of that finale had been on the screens on March 18, 1999, two seniors in Littleton, Colorado, walked into Columbine High School armed with guns and bombs and began a reign of destruction that killed a number of their classmates.

That it was a tragedy was beyond debate. The loss of life was terrible—and this was real life, not a television fiction. People had died before they had a chance to realize their goals in life, before they'd had a chance to become adults. The real reasons the two did it might never be known, but it justifiably caused anger in the nation about the access of teens to weapons, and also about the prevalence of violence in films and television.

There was violence on *Buffy*, even if it was generally directed against demons, monsters, and vampires. Buffy was, after all, a *Slayer*, so it was a part of her very nature. But with a nation in mourning, the airing of the season's climax the following week would have been in very poor taste. The decision was taken at the network to postpone it until feelings had died down, and it was something that won indirect praise from President Clinton in a speech he made.

Yes, it ruined the whole story arc, in a way, but there were greater issues at stake here, and the people at WB had at least made a gesture.

In the end, it would be July 13 that the second part of the finale aired, although rumor had it that bootleg tapes of the episode had begun circulating among fans almost as soon as the decision to postpone had been taken.

It wasn't a publicity ruse to garner more viewers for the finale, although a few cynics might have deemed it so. It was a genuine, well-meant gesture.

"It wasn't necessary," says Joss Whedon, "but I understand the instinct behind it and certainly wouldn't argue with the motivation."

In *TV Guide*, critic Matt Roush pointed out that airing the episode on its original date, given that the students would be wielding crossbows in an attempt to defeat the demons, "might have demonized *Buffy*" (pun not intended). And it's true that some people would have read much more into the episode than Whedon (who had written and directed the finale) had ever intended.

In the aftermath of the violent climax Buffy and Angel looked at each other from a distance. Smoke

and mist swirled, and Angel vanished from Sunnydale, simply walking away.

For a finale that had been so widely publicized, it
was a bit of a disappointment. There was the obvious
image of blowing up your high school, which so many
students have wanted to do, and the idea of high
school as a battle—that was the teenage element of it
all. The blood union between Angel and Buffy was
the more adult side, in some ways, while still remain-
ing romantic. It was a shame, though, that there was
more recourse to action, rather than words—language
had always been the series' strong point—but it was,
perhaps, necessary.

But the amount of fighting, and the explosion,
made it apparent why network officials had decided
to postpone airing the episode.

Notably, after the show's conclusion, the WB aired
a promotional spot for *Angel*, just in case any *Buffy*
fan didn't know the show would be starting this fall.

In the end, although Angel was one of the season's
main characters within the show, he wasn't as involved as he had been in season two. Having gone to
great lengths to bring him into the fold, which made
his change and his trip to hell all the more shocking,
the writers now kept him separate from the rest of the
Scooby Gang. When he was seen, it was all too often
just with Buffy, exploring the changing nature of their
relationship and he slowly healed and practiced his tai
chi.

That sense of separation was important from a
long-term fictional standpoint. With the end of this
season, there would be no more Angel on *Buffy*, so it
was as much a process of weaning away as anything

else, establishing him as a character who would be able to function without the others. Both he, and the show's viewers, had been brought to terms with his past, in which he atoned for his sins, but some divine force wasn't willing to let him kill himself.

Notably, in the two-part season finale, Angel was the weak one, the one who'd been poisoned, and it was up to Buffy to save him. During the first two seasons he'd been strong, no matter whether he was good or bad. But this season it was Buffy who'd helped bring him back from hell (it was implied that her love had saved him, even if that idea was never explicitly stated), and who'd taken part in his physical rehabilitation. Now she would be the one to save him from a rather ugly death by poisoning.

What we'd been given, essentially, was a softer picture of Angel, a completely different facet opened up, making him far more human and vulnerable—and, in other words, making the character ready to be spun off into his own series. It probably hadn't seemed that way, experiencing each story individually, but looking back at the arc of things, and the tone, that certainly seemed to be the way it had been intended. And it was fair enough. Having brought Angel back from hell, the writers had to do something with him, something that would make him different from the ways he'd been before.

And that final, delayed farewell to Sunnydale, on July 13, 1999, meant that David had to be prepared to turn it all up two or three notches. The Scooby Gang were moving on with their lives, and Angel had to move on with his. He'd loved Buffy a long time, as he'd told her earlier in the season, right from the moment he'd first seen her in Los Angeles, well before Sunnydale. But even the ultimate forbidden love couldn't remain static, and together there was absolutely nowhere else they could go.

CHAPTER TEN

AND

so it was time to leave Sunnydale and *Buffy*, and move on to other pastures. *Angel*, as the show was tentatively called, would be set in Los Angeles, a place full of many kinds of demons.

It would be the first spinoff from *BTVS*, a show that would undergo some changes itself as the gang split up for college. The older presence of Angel, who was certainly no teenager, meant that the show was likely to be more adult, according to Joss Whedon, who, apart from being creator, would also be executive producer.

"It's more of an anthology show than *Buffy*," Whedon explains. "There's not a soap opera at the center of it."

There was a big difference between being a major supporting character in a series to having a character take on his own series, and Whedon was well aware of those problems.

"We want to find the humor in *Angel* and not have it be some dark dullathon. We've played [Angel] very brooding, and we've seen his evil side, but his humor is starting to come out," David says. "It's dry and sarcastic, very subtle. It's not a way-out kind of humor."

There would still be a great deal of darkness to the show, however; that was pretty much Angel's trademark—the black clothes, the life in shadows. To have a workable show, though, you needed a premise on which to build it. For *Angel*, that started out quite nebulous. In L.A., David says, Angel will "fight the inner demons of everybody. I want to take [them] off everybody else's shoulders. It's almost like a cure for humanity."

And it sounded like a big job, even for a member of the undead. Being so open-ended meant there could be many possibilities, which could be good, but also had the possibility of leaving the show unfocused. There was plenty of talk of characters from *Buffy* making guest appearances on the new show, but it was finally revealed that one of the regulars—Charisma Carpenter, who plays Cordelia Chase, would become part of the cast of *Angel*.

"Actually, I'm looking forward to it with open arms and open heart," enthuses Carpenter. "I'm very excited about it. It sounds like it's going to appeal to an older audience, which is exciting. Also, I'm looking forward to spending more time working with David because he's a really talented actor and I don't get the pleasure of working with him too often."

The character of Cordelia had softened over three seasons. From being a rather cheap foil for Buffy and the Slayerettes, she'd become quite three-dimensional, and an accepted member of the crew. Still, she was somewhat spoiled and naturally a tad shallow. But advance word on *Angel* has it that Cordelia will no longer be quite the same. Her family will lose its money, and Cordelia will be in the City of Angels not as a little rich girl, a Trust fund kid, but somone learning how to make ends meet—financially and emotionally.

There were also unconfirmed rumors that the Slayer, Faith (Eliza Dushku) and the witch, Amy (Elizabeth Anne Allen) would join the cast of the new show, which would mean a great deal of crossover, and enough in the way of female characters to draw in an adoring male, as well as female, audience. As *SFX* magazine pointed out humorously, having three women in, working with Angel, offered some echoes of the seventies show *Charlie's Angels*. But there would also be the lighter presence of a character named Doyle, played by Glenn Quinn, who'd portrayed Becky's husband on *Roseanne*, another member of the undead, but one completely different to Angel.

"The higher powers have called Doyle to be Angel's guide, and he's the last person in the world who wants to—or should—be doing this. He really just wants to play the ponies and drink a lot. But he has unexpected wisdom in the midst of his extreme foibles."

However, David says, "it will hopefully be able to attract an older audience. We'll be able to do things on the show that we won't or couldn't get away with on *Buffy*. Older things, cooler things, because it'll definitely be a different time slot. It'll be more graphic. This series has more adult content that Joss wants to explore."

That said, it wasn't going to be another *Millennium* (the show created by Chris Carter of *X-Files* fame), where the darkness was unrelenting, and each week the hero went in pursuit of another killer. What truly separates Angel from other television leading men is the fact that he's a vampire—not the first and probably not the last—and a vampire who's balanced on a knife-edge. He can be good, and he can also be bad, and in this new series he would be able to use both aspects of himself. As David explains it, "He'll take the soul or save the soul, depending on the situation. It's moving on to a different level, a different look, and a different show, but the same kind of premises."

While the show came from Joss Whedon's mind (and his clout), given the success of *Buffy*, the writing would be from the pen of David Greenwalt, who'd worked with Whedon on *BTVS*, where he wrote and directed three episodes. Whedon described the basic idea for the show as *"Touched by an Equalizer,"* a neat shorthand reference to two television shows: the somewhat saccharine *Touched by an Angel* and the old show, *The Equalizer*, which starred Edward Woodward as a man who obtained justice for those who'd been wronged.

It would be wrong to think it'll all be black or white, however. With its relatively dark atmosphere, there would more likely be moral shades of gray. At the same time, however, it wouldn't be wallowing in angst. So what did all this add up to? Basically, a very difficult time for writers and crew, to focus and sustain the vision without it dipping into something less than entertaining.

What it has going for it, apart from David, is the track record of *Buffy*, and starting out with some strong characters. But, like any new series, even one spun off from a successful show, it's something of a crapshoot as to whether it'll find favor with the public. But it's a gamble that's worth taking, if only to see David blossom when he's given more room to act.

And there'd be ample opportunity for that as things developed, at least within Whedon's plans.

"I see [*Angel*] as the second half of *Buffy*," he explains. "We deal a lot with addiction as a metaphor, because that's Angel. He's sort of a reformed drunk, so he's fighting his way back to something resembling humanity and helping others do the same."

As the time came closer to begin production on *Angel*, which set up shop for filming its first episodes in June 1999, it became apparent that, in spite of earlier rumors, there'd be little in the way of characters crossing over between *Angel* and *Buffy*. The logistics made it too difficult; each of the main characters would be too involved in their shows (Buffy, Willow, Giles, and Xander in *Buffy*, Angel and Cordelia in *Angel*) to have the time to do more work. At the same time, the producers weren't ruling out the possibility of it happening occasionally. But one thing that had been ruled out, at least in the short term, was any romance between Angel and Cordy, and that was all for the best. Apart from the fact that it would have seemed strained, a deliberate device, it wouldn't have worked. Angel's intensity could never have lined up with Cordelia's more vacuous world view. Besides, with Cordelia's track record in romances, it would have been unlikely to go very far.

There was no mention of any romance on the show, although it was bound to rear its head at some point along the line. None of the characters could be so completely focused on work as to make it their entire lives, and the way that worked with *Buffy* was to flesh out the main players, to help them become three-dimensional. It seemed impossible that Greenwalt would forget that lesson—or that Whedon would let him. But as to where anything might go, and who the objects of the romances might be, either no one knew yet, or no one was saying.

One thing that *was* for certain was that *Angel* was one of the most anticipated new shows of the 1999–2000 television season. To call it TV for the millennium might seem trite, but it was probably apt. The popularity of shows like *X-Files*, *Millennium*, and *Buffy the Vampire Slayer* as the century clicked to an end certainly indicated that the public was preoccupied with something even if it was only subconsciously. There were monsters out there, even if they only existed in our heads, but we felt the need to explore them, to face our fears, in a way, before we could move on to the freshness of a new thousand years.

For it does seem as if people think that a new millennium will wipe the slate clean, as if all the bad things of the past will be washed away once the clock strikes midnight to usher in 2000 (or 2001, depending on when you believe the next century begins). That might seem like a simplistic view, but at some level it has been held by a number of people, as if all their preoccupations and thoughts would suddenly change.

Were that to be the case, then it would spell the death of a number of television shows in the ratings—which would seem unlikely. Neither *Buffy* nor *Angel* (which would have the advantage of starting with a built in audience of *Buffy* fans) would likely be going off the air anytime soon.

The WB network had grown since *Buffy the Vampire Slayer* first hit the airwaves. Building on the success of that show, there had been *Dawson's Creek* and *Felicity*, which marked the upstart as speaking directly to—rather than at—teens, in a way that Fox hadn't even managed in its early days. While *Angel* aspired to be more adult than that, there was little doubt that its initial audience (and many of the hardcore David Boreanaz fans) would draw from that same pool. Obviously not all, however, as David had discovered on his Levi's promotional tour. He hadn't quite known what to expect in terms of people coming to see him, but he'd been astonished by the age range.

"It's really been across the board," he said at the time. "It's been young kids, teenagers, anywhere up to people in their forties and fifties. One older guy camped out at six in the morning in Boston. It just ranges. And a lot of housewives."

That was his constituency. Over the second and third season, through great reviews and word-of-mouth, *Buffy* had attracted a much wider range of viewers, many of whom had stuck with the show as it developed. While some of those hoped to see the magic between Buffy and Angel reignited, the chances of that happening were somewhere between slim and none. That had been fully established in the third season, after Angel's return from hell. Besides, in the fourth season of *BTVS*, the writers were planning a new romantic interest for Buffy, in the form of Riley Finn, a freshman in her college class, which one magazine described as "Clark Kent to Angel's Bruce Wayne," i.e. good as opposed to dark. So while Angel and Buffy might remain the great loves of each other's lives, it would be one romance that was never built to last. Perhaps that was a shame, given that it was one of the great screen love affairs (be it large or small screen), doomed from the beginning, but utterly compelling. Obviously, Angel wasn't going to find anyone like her again (and the idea of Angel getting together with another Slayer, Faith, seemed as if it wouldn't work from the word go). But the romance, as well as his history, had really helped Angel stick in the minds of viewers, and helped him become a tragic figure—of which there are far too few on television.

While he might have originally become a vampire because he gave in to his temptations and his flesh was weak, and while he might have wreaked a path of death and destruction across Europe, Angel had helped pay for his sins. And it was love—a very human ideal—that had lifted his curse, and sent him off roaring again. Even then, he'd never fully lost the love of a good woman. For Angel to fall again, it would have to be with someone who measured up to the standards of Buffy—and that wasn't going to be easy to find.

And, if it happened, it would never be the focus of the show.

Really, the show pivoted on David's abilities as an actor. There would be strong plots and characters, but so much depended on his portrayal of Angel. To simply brood was not going to be enough. Angel would have to expand in every way.

"I think he'll be able to tap into his evil side and control it, rather than go out of bounds with it," David says. "So he'll be a combination of [good and evil], which should be cool. But he won't be killing—or he might kill some people, you never know. If *Buffy*'s a show about adolescence, I think Angel's show will be about renewal of one's self esteem, and what [his] purpose is all about in life."

In other words, as Joss Whedon said, *Touched by*

an Equalizer. There was no doubt that shows with a New Age-y, feel-good aspect had done well on television, and an intelligent action series would always have a home in prime time. But few had managed to combine the two before. Certainly, the more philosophical aspect fit in well with David's personality. But it was a fine line to walk. You couldn't have Angel change too much, or those who adored him would find him unbelievable, nor could he be a killing machine. Following the events in Littleton, Colorado, the issue of violence on television and at the movies had come under much greater scrutiny. Nor was violence necessarily an answer to everything, as Whedon, David, and everyone involved with the show understood. There might be times within the story line when it was necessary, and came as justice, but it wouldn't be a slugfest. That had never quite been Angel's style, anyway.

Much of Angel's drama had always been internal, the conflicts that existed within himself, and trying to conquer his own demons. The portrayal of that had taken place within the story lines of *Buffy*; would it be possible to show them in the same way in *Angel*? That was certainly one of the challenges facing David Greenwalt. And if it wasn't done like that, what would they do? Again, that was something to be decided, one of the joys and pains of writing a new series.

Something that had to be considered was what made Angel such a popular character. Obviously, a great part of his appeal was David himself, the man behind the mask, as it were. He had the looks, the body, and the acting ability. Visually, he was the person to whom viewers responded. But there was more going on.

Essentially, although Angel was a vampire, he did represent some kind of ideal, a man who was very much in touch with all the parts of his nature and his personality. There might have been times when that wasn't so, but at the beginning and the end of his appearances on *Buffy the Vampire Slayer*, that was definitely the case. Men are notorious for not displaying their emotions and not talking about them. While Angel might not have discussed his feelings very much, they were all too apparent on his face and in his actions. When he was angry, his vampire face appeared, and then he could become violent—and his force was quick and very decisive; it wasn't violence for its own sake, but because he was pushed into it. It wasn't something he could turn off. And he was very protective of the girl he loved—as long as he was involved, he'd do everything in his power (which was a great deal) to ensure that nothing bad happened to his lover. On top of that, he was quite learned—although how anyone could reach some two and a half centuries in age and not have learned a few things would have been a bigger mystery. He *knew* things, not just about life, but about the occult, and that certainly tapped into his mystery factor.

While Angel couldn't help but show some of his emotions, other parts of him remained hidden depths. You could never completely get a handle on him; there was always going to be something of an enigma. Even Buffy would never have had the chance to understand him completely, except on an intuitive level. When you thought he'd revealed a little more, a peek underneath would show it was just another layer, and getting to the core of him was almost impossible. Indeed, there'd only been one person who'd ever had a chance of doing that: Buffy.

While he had his aggressive side, Angel could also be tender. You could say that he was confident enough of his own strength to be free to show that. Obviously, Buffy was the one who saw it most, but there were flashes of it on display to others, too.

The idea, basically, was that Angel was a man with a lot of his characteristics exaggerated. He was extremely in touch with his animal side—which was the violent, animal aspect of his personality. And it wasn't always under his control when the animal would be unleashed. To some, that side of him was very appealing. It meant he was close to nature, that the veneer of civilization on him was actually quite thin. Of course, the animal was a vampire—not really an animal at all—but that was somehow beside the point. He reacted when it was necessary, not just for the fun of it, which meant that there was a reason for his violence. The cursed Angel never hurt or took the life of a good guy.

And in his most tender moments, Angel was very, very romantic, which again, held a great deal of appeal. He could have been almost seductive in his charm, if he'd wanted to be. But that wouldn't have been his style. Angel was completely honest. He might have courted Buffy, but he'd never have attempted to seduce her, because there would have been an inherent dishonesty about such an action.

The fact that Angel had no time for the games that so often go on into relationships made him more appealing to women. Although he could be jealous, when he was "himself" he never tried to mess with Buffy's head, to play mind games with her. He loved her, and that was that. He was loyal, even devoted to her, and that was never in doubt for a second. There had been no hurry for them to consummate their relationship; he'd been more than happy for her to move along at a pace that was comfortable for her, rather than try and force things. In other words, in matters of romance, he was a complete gentleman, something most men—and particularly most teenage males—simply aren't. Deception wasn't a part of who he was, on any level.

That innate honesty fitted in with the idea of him being close to the animal side of his personality. With an animal, what you see is what you get—they don't play tricks on you. And that sense of wildness just below the surface can hold a very definite attraction, with its sense of the untamed. While Angel didn't have a job (at least, not in the generally accepted sense of the term) or money, it would have been impossible to imagine him working nine to five in an office and then going home to a suburban ranch house and worrying about paying all his bills. Apart from the fact that it wouldn't have worked, there was no way it would have fit with the character.

The fact that Angel dressed predominantly in dark colors, mostly black, was a reflection of the fact that he was, at heart, somewhat antiestablishment (within the arts and music, where people see themselves, usually wrongly, as outside society, black clothing is almost de rigueur). And while David would have loved to have seen his character spending time with vampire friends (which would have probably assumed there were other "reformed" vampires), Angel was very much a loner. He lived by himself. The vast majority of time was spent on his own. All of which served to

increase the sense of mystery about him. Loners become that way for a few reasons. Sometimes no one
wants to know them, they want to shun society, or
they have problems that stop them getting emotionally
close to anyone. While Angel had elements of all
three factors, none of them adequately described him.
He kept his distance by choice, but he could get close
to Buffy. He could, from time to time, even open up
a little to people.

That distance between Angel and the rest of the
world heightened the romantic aspect of his character,
as if he was carrying a huge weight on his shoulders
(which he was—guilt). And the mysterious, romantic
loner has always been a character with a lot of allure.
People think they might be the one to lift his burden,
to pierce the defenses and bring him back into the
mainstream of society.

It was particularly interesting that Angel was sent
to Hell to atone for his sins after he turned back into
a "real" vampire. That a mortal could send someone
there (and somehow seem instrumental in bringing
him back later) was literally fantastic. But the very
nature of *Buffy*, where the fantastic seemed to happen
every day without anyone batting an eyelid, put it in
almost a parallel universe. Certain parts of California
might have been used to strange occurrences, but on-
slaughts of demons and vampires weren't among
them! So for Angel to come back from Hell, while a
surprise, was accepted. Hell, of course, was purely a
Christian shorthand for a place to go and pay for
sins—within the religion proper, Hell is for damna-
tion and eternity, not simply a short period.

Given that Angel's return happened after there'd
been an announcement that he'd be getting his own

series, the fact that he was then shown as more vulnerable, not the kind of superman he'd been earlier, indicated a rounding of his character. For all intents and purposes, it made him more human, and somewhat less detached. He relied more on others, most particularly Buffy. Their relationship might have changed somewhat, but she was still willing to help him, in any way she could, and offer him all she had. And Angel was open enough, in touch with himself enough, to allow her to do that.

Adding vulnerability to the arsenal of Angel more or less completed the picture of him as something of an ideal man. He could be compared to boyfriends and husbands, and the men in real life would be somehow found wanting. Not just physically, but in many ways. It was a subtle idealization, and the subtext—that Angel, it had to be remembered, was a vampire—meant that one could safely say it would be impossible to find anyone quite as perfect in real life.

While many would project Angel's personality onto David, he would be the first to point out that he really wasn't Angel. It had taken him some time to find and become comfortable with himself. Angel was just a character he played on television. It might fill his thoughts for most of his waking hours, but there was a huge distinction between fiction and life. While appealing to large numbers of people had made David into a star, he had no wish to model himself on Angel, and it would serve his fans well to make the distinction, too.

It had all led to this, to a soundstage, and work on a show where he was the star. Things had come together exactly as they should. A strong, excellent actor, who also happened to be extremely good-looking and buff, playing a character that was almost the perfect creation. It all promised to be magic.

Inevitably, the show would take a few weeks to really find its feet, and Whedon had lobbied WB entertainment president Susanne Daniels to have *Angel* follow *Buffy* on Tuesday nights. It was an idea that made eminent sense. One really did carry on from the other, and it would help keep the same audience viewing for another hour, which would considerably help *Angel* as it started (Daniels wanted that time slot for *Angel* as well, but told Whedon it wasn't carved in stone. His response was to send her a stone with "Angel, Tuesdays at 9" carved into it). And that was the way it would end up being.

Of course, that assumed that the show would need help. The likelihood is that it will do well, and be able to stand strongly on his own. Angel has become fully and firmly established as a character over the course of three seasons with *Buffy*, and David has acquired a legion of fans, who'll happily follow him. Nor will it detract from the *Buffy* legend; if anything, it'll add to it. For a show to be big enough to warrant a spinoff, it has to have achieved a certain status, whether in terms of viewing numbers or critical cachet, and *Buffy* definitely has the latter. For a growing number, it remains appointment television, and *Angel* will be the same way. David, as he's shown, is strong enough (and with broad enough shoulders, as many would gladly point out) to carry his own series. The acting team is fine, and David Greenwalt has enough of a record with *Buffy* to be trusted. And then, of course, there's Joss Whedon, who's not likely to let anything substandard go out under his name. It's worth remembering that the initial vision for Angel, the character, was his, and that he remains the mastermind behind the new show. David might be the realization, but without Whedon it would never have happened at all.

It's the biggest leap of David's life, but it's safe to say that he's ready for it. He's been working a long time for something like this to happen, and he appreciates the value of it all. When he first won the role of Angel, no one imagined it would all come to this, least of all David himself. But as much as any writer or producer, he made it happen. It was his face, and his talent, that brought Angel to life, and made him touch people. He has the power in his hands, and he's determined to exercise it cautiously and wisely.

The position he's in now brings a lot of responsibility, something of which he's quite well aware. A lot of other people are depending on his name and drawing power for their jobs, which isn't the easiest situation to be in, especially since success is largely out of his hands. However, he does have faith that it will all work out. If it didn't feel right, he wouldn't be doing it.

Every actor, every creative person, has to have a large ego. They have to feel that no one else can do what they do, certainly not in quite the same way, nor as well. But there's a difference between the confidence a performer needs, and cockiness. David has never been troubled by the latter, nor is he ever likely to be. He's driven as an actor, but not as a star. Any stardom that's happened has been something he's had to live with, not that he's actively sought. But it's here, and it's simply going to become more intense.

David has ridden the flow to his own series. Obviously, the talent and personality have to be there, but luck has played its part. Angel has been the right character at the right time, and *Buffy* has been the right series to strike a chord with the type of audience all networks want.

The biggest worry is getting a consistent time slot for the show, and not having it being preempted too often. *Angel* might start up with a built-in audience, but it will need to develop its own following. As long as it stays at one day and time—where people can easily find it from week to week—the chances are it will emulate *Buffy*'s success. If the network starts moving it around, different days, different times, then that will be the kiss of death, the equivalent of an executive coming after it with a wooden stake.

The expectations will be high for the series. After all, not only is Angel a proven character, but Joss Whedon will be piggybacking on a success. There'll be ample publicity and advertising to let people know the show will be on. The payback the network will want for that is numbers—a large amount of viewers tuning in, not just the first or second week, but *every* week. The pressure is on, not only to make a show as good as *Buffy* (which means recapture that special something that sets the show apart), but to keep viewers, preferably more and more of them, coming back every week.

How do you do that? If there was a formula for it, then every new show would be a hit. The truth is that the vast majority of new shows flop. They're canceled within a matter of weeks. The main thing the networks seem to do is throw stuff against a wall and see what sticks. Not very scientific, but after all these years, it's still the best they've come up with.

No one knows what makes one show a hit and another a failure. All anyone can do is hope, and probably pray that they still have a job the following season.

But, going into the scariest time, right before the ringing in of the millennium, the chances for *Angel* look very good. Of course, a lot can go wrong, but the signs are all very strong that it could be one of the winners in the new season. Everyone involved in the show was completely committed to it, and willing to do everything to make it a success. They were willing to work the long hours, to continually strive to make it better, to compete.

While all the elements are very positive, the show will ultimately rest with David and Angel. We already know the character, and David's acting, is compelling when he works as part of an ensemble. Now, heading one, he faces his biggest-ever challenge. He can't let his concentration slip for one second, and he has to be aware, not only of his own part, but of everything else that's going on around him.

Can he do it? Of course he can. With Angel he seems to have a touch that's pure magic. He has a face that resonates with large numbers of the female population, and a character that can encompass a wide range of emotions (he might have shown his brooding and romantic sides a great deal in the past, but be prepared for much, much more). He's the kind of man a lot of women wish they had in their lives—although, in reality, they might find him a bit too much for them.

And David is grounded enough to make it all work, to see it all comes together. He's ambitious as an actor, but not in terms of career. This isn't merely a stepping stone to a series of movie roles for him—it's an end in itself. And that means he'll do everything in his power to make it the very best it can be.

Very few really know the future. But it would be a reasonable bet to wager on the success of *Angel*. Some things, as David himself might tell you, simply feel right. And if it didn't feel right, he wouldn't undertake it. But Angel hasn't just returned from Hell, he's come fully alive, and developed into someone with passion, and a hunger that isn't going to be fed by blood.

Always, it's up to the viewers, to people like you, as to whether a show lasts. You hold the power in your remote. But you also hold the power in the recommendations you can make to other people. If you like what you see, tell your friends, remind them to watch. That's a bigger factor than any kind of advertising.

These days, it's only the suits at the network who have the power to kill *Angel*. But it's people like you who have the power to keep him alive. It won't be forever, since each show has a lifespan that evolves and ends, but long enough for him to remain strong—in memory and eventually in reruns.

CHAPTER ELEVEN

OF all the regular characters on *Buffy the Vampire Slayer*, a team made up of Angel and Cordelia would have seemed the least likely. If anything, they seemed complete opposites. He was the dark character who often didn't need words to express himself. She, on the other hand, often spoke before she thought, and ended up with her foot in her mouth.

So why, one had to wonder, would Cordelia Chase become a regular cast member of *Angel*?

To be fair, Los Angeles was perfect for Cordy. With all the clothes and shoe stores her heart could desire, it would be like an entry into Paradise for her, even if her taste in clothes did often run toward the conservative.

But the Cordelia who would arrive in L.A. would be somewhat different from the one who'd been a part of the regular cast of *Buffy*. There she'd been the spoiled child of rich parents, somewhat vacuous, although she'd developed from the archetypal airhead as the series progressed. Now, it seemed her family would lose its money, and Cordelia would be dependent on herself for survival.

Given that she'd have a large role in the series, it

seemed unlikely that she'd be there purely for comic relief, although that was how she'd appeared in the early days of *Buffy*. But her character had acquired a certain depth, making her less of a cartoon and into a person with three very real dimensions. Undoubtedly, in her new financial adversity, Cordelia would grow a great deal, and very quickly.

For all that, though, Angel and Cordelia seemed a very unusual and unlikely pairing. But perhaps that was the whole point. Almost since the inception of television, shows had used unlikely pairings to create sparks and tension. Although it was a sitcom, the whole premise of *The Odd Couple* was the clash of personalities between the two leads, and it had since become a feature in other comedies and dramas, with the more lightweight character being the sidekick. So *Angel* would actually be drawing on a rich TV tradition in this.

But in many ways, *Angel*, like *Buffy*, wouldn't be a traditional show, so there were likely to be major twists on the formula. Not that Cordelia was likely to turn into a rocket scientist or an expert on the occult overnight, but there would probably be some big changes in her worldview. Maybe not all at once, but over the course of a season or two.

For Charisma Carpenter, who plays Cordelia, this will be a challenge to relish. In *Buffy*, as she acknowledged, she and David rarely had scenes together, so what kind of sparks they generate remains to be seen. But it's almost inevitable that the protected, somewhat naive Cordy will be forced to grow up at a rapid pace, even if it won't always be easy for her.

If anything, it'll make the character a bit more like the actress who portrays her. Like David with Angel,

Charisma has little in common with Cordelia; quite the opposite, in fact. Acting involves three things more or less lacking from Cordelia's life—intelligence, empathy, and focus.

In fact, Charisma originally auditioned for the role of Buffy, before Sarah Michelle Gellar entered the picture, although, at the same time, she was asked to read for Cordelia, the part she eventually won. To anyone familiar with the show, the idea of Charisma as Buffy might seem impossible, but it almost happened.

Charisma had been involved in the performing arts since she was five years old, when she began formally studying ballet. However, her entrance into acting was almost as accidental as David's. She was living in Los Angeles, and waitressing for a living at Mirabelle on Sunset—one of the main alternative professions for aspiring actresses. Her intention, however, was to save money to return to college, where she could finish her degree and become an English teacher. Not too surprisingly, given her looks, patrons at the restaurant assumed she was an actress or a model. Finally she was introduced to an agent. He recommended she take acting classes, and she began studying at the highly reputable Playhouse West for eighteen months.

"That was where I discovered how much I enjoyed acting and what an outlet it was—and that I could make money at it," she says.

Making a living from her art wasn't something that had occurred to Charisma (she's named after an Avon scent popular in the 1970s, when she was born) earlier. She'd been born (on July 23, 1970) and raised in Las Vegas. From the time she began ballet, it had been an avocation for her. Even a stomach injury that came the year she began dancing could put her off being active.

The young Charisma had gone where she shouldn't—into the backyard while the pool was being built. Like any young kid, she was attracted by the forbidden. That it was dangerous only made it more enticing. She fell and impaled herself on some reinforcing bars. It was a serious injury, although in the end she only needed stitches, which left a scar on her stomach (and so you don't find Cordelia wearing too many middy outfits).

Once the injury had healed, there were no lingering side effects, and her movement wasn't restricted, so Charisma was able to continue her dance. And continue she did. All the way through childhood she continued to study ballet. As an adolescent, too, her training continued, helped in great part by the talent she showed. When she was fifteen, her family moved to Mexico (actually just south of the U.S.), and Charisma made a daily commute across the border to San Diego where she took her classes at the School of the Creative and Performing Arts.

Obviously, in ballet, talent alone doesn't spell success, but it wasn't a career that Charisma was interested in pursuing. It was purely for her own satisfaction. However, the high school did offer a good education, one that would leave her well-prepared for college, although, by her own account, Charisma wasn't very academic. Nor, unlike Cordelia, was she part of the popular clique. In fact, she was quite the loner, one whose days seemed to devolve around her dance classes more than anything else. She did have a wild side, though, which was fostered by her Harley-riding uncles—and there was also the time she "borrowed" her father's Corvette without first asking permission.

That wasn't where she was bound on graduation, however. Instead, she took a different, but fairly well-trodden path, heading to Europe to do some traveling, take some time to consider what she really wanted, and just to live a little away from the rigors of academics.

It was a time of freedom for Charisma, one that helped her grow a lot, learning to survive on her own in foreign countries, where the culture and the language were very different. After several months away she returned a much more adult person, with definite ideas of what she wanted from her life. The main one was to become a teacher, and most specifically an English teacher—which would have gladdened the hearts of many high-school boys if she'd actually followed through on it.

Initially, she enrolled in junior college in San Diego, supporting herself by waitressing, then working in a video store, anything to help pay her tuition. Junior college, of course, was just a two-year program, giving her an associate degree. Once she'd completed that, rather than immediately enter the university system and work toward her bachelor's degree, she took more time to mass her own college fund. And that meant wore working. First of all she was an aerobics instructor, after which, in 1991, she became one of the cheerleaders for the San Diego Chargers. For both jobs, her dance background would prove to be a huge plus, since she not only moved well, but was very fit.

It was after her stint as a cheerleader (a job Cordelia would probably have envied) that she headed north to L.A. and discovery, even though that wasn't her initial plan. After falling in love with acting, though, there was no turning back, and once she'd completed her training at Playhouse West, she was ready to dive in at the deep end.

Initially, she made her living appearing in television commercials—she'd end up doing more than twenty of them—the best-known being an ad for Secret antiperspirant, which aired for more than two years. Maybe it wasn't the kind of role she'd envisioned while studying acting, but it paid the bills quite well.

From commercials she did manage to snag a role on one of the highest-rated syndicated shows, when she made a guest appearance on *Baywatch* (or *Babewatch* as many of its fans called the show). Whether it was high art or not was irrelevant—every week a lot of people tuned in to see it, and Charisma had a chance to make an impact. And that was exactly what she did.

Aaron Spelling had a track record as one of television's most successful producers—his work included *Charlie's Angels* and *Beverly Hills 90210*—and for more than twenty years he'd been bringing forth hits. So when he began work on a new show, there was a great deal of interest. From her work on *Baywatch*, Charisma auditioned, and soon found herself with a role in Spelling's new show, *Malibu Shores*.

Even the most successful producer can't hit a home run every time, and that was the way it seemed with *Malibu Shores*. The ratings simply weren't there. For whatever reason, people just didn't want to know about it.

"Working with Aaron Spelling was a great experience," says Charisma. "But I was working on his show, and the vibe was that it wasn't 'going.' Thankfully, my agent sent me out on the *Buffy the Vampire Slayer* audition."

While other girls turned up for the audition dressed to kill (which could have been apt, given the role they were auditioning for), Charisma took a different tack—one that let the producers know she believed Buffy would be her own girl, not a relentless follower of fashion.

"So I auditioned wearing overalls, a leather jacket and flip flops. It was a really bizarre day. Joss Whedon was there and I didn't know [the audition] was for producers only."

With her background in dance and movement, Charisma had no doubt she could master the very physical part of Buffy. The producers, though, seemed to have different ideas. "Then they wanted me to read for Cordelia five minutes later. I did, and I guess they really liked it."

It wasn't what she'd expected, and initially she wasn't prepared for it. She was given a quarter of an hour to prepare herself, and obviously, whatever she did worked very well.

Whatever disappointment she might have felt at not winning the lead in the upcoming series was at least tempered by the fact that she walked away with a part. Well, at that point she'd *almost* walked away with the part. There was still the screen test, and that was where things almost went horribly wrong.

She was still working on *Malibu Shores* at the time and had to travel from Malibu to Burbank in the notorious Los Angeles traffic. The rain was coming down, cars were moving slowly, and Charisma was running late, although it wasn't her fault. Finally, her agent paged her, and when she answered, he told her that she needed to hurry up—the crew was about to leave.

"I said, 'You tell them that they'd better order a pizza or something, because I did not drive an hour and a half in traffic to not go in there and at least audition.' Obviously, I was panicked."

All was well that ended well. The screen test seemed to go smoothly, everyone laughing off Charisma's delayed entrance, and she truly felt it was all wrapped up.

And it was.

Initially, Cordelia Chase was the kind of high school girl who courted popularity and popular people. Every school has them, the type that cuts you dead if you're not part of the "right" circle. She was a bitch and an airhead, and perfectly happy with the way she was living her life, oblivious to all the things going on around her. Other than light relief, she seemed to serve no purpose on the show. It wasn't a role that offered a lot of challenge to an actress. As Charisma noted of Cordelia back then, "She's always looking for attention and never getting it, and it's irritating to her. The fan mail is disheartening, too, saying things like 'Are you ever going to be nice?' My response is, 'I *am* nice. They're meaner to me than I am to them.' "

That certainly did seem to be true, in many ways. Cordelia was the butt of many of the Slayerettes' jokes, the lightweight who seemed to stumble through life while they were engaged in serious business.

Between the first and second seasons, however, there was a change, as Cordelia was brought into the fold of the Scooby Gang. Maybe not quite *all* the way, but enough to be a part of things.

"I wasn't sure how I felt about it because I didn't want to lose my edge," she says. "I didn't want her to be nice; I didn't want her to change because that's who she is."

But Cordelia didn't change *too* much. And while she was now a Slayerette, she was still more or less Little Miss Hapless.

"I asked Joss why I'm not more involved with the group when they're off digging up bodies, because I think there are potentially a lot of funny things that would have come out of that. He said, 'We have to get you out there so you can be kidnaped and be the victim.' "

The "new" Cordelia had to be taken somewhat more seriously. Within the fairly rigid hierarchy of high school, she'd lost a lot of her standing by aligning herself with the Slayerettes, who made very little attempt to ingratiate themselves with the popular kids. And when she began dating Xander, she lost all stature in the group. That was fine, however; Cordelia was finally discovering herself as an individual, even if Xander was someone totally different from her, and it was a romance that was doomed to only flicker briefly.

By giving Cordelia more resonance, she became more three-dimensional, and far less of a stereotype. To keep her as part of the show, that was more or less a necessity, although many of the familiar traits remained in place. She was still someone who tended to speak before thinking, and to say exactly what was on her mind, whether it offended anyone or not. Tact was definitely not her long suit. And after a while, what had been annoying became somewhat endearing. Cordy (as she became accepted, the nickname was used, indicating she was now a full part of the Gang) could be relied upon to point out the faults in all manner of plans and people. That she hadn't changed too much was rather reassuring. It meant a few things could be relied upon in the universe. And she was willing to pitch in and help the others when asked—albeit often reluctantly—in various projects, as long as they didn't involve getting messy or dirty. She might no longer have been part of the popular clique, but she still had standards. And she still expected to be given a lot of latitude because of who she was, although the spoiled brat quotient of her personality was gradually diminishing, and Cordy was proving she could have some original thoughts, even if they weren't all good—such as her brief desire for the geekish Watcher, Wesley.

By the end of *Buffy's* third season, Cordelia had become as beloved as any other regular cast member. Yes, she was goofy, but she was no longer a bitch, as she had been a couple of years before. She was growing up and, apparently, moving on. Charisma had urged the producers in the past to make her character meaner, if only to differentiate her from the overall niceness of the others, but they hadn't really done so—which was probably all for the best, in the long run. In many ways, she was the most disposable character of all the regulars. Each of the others contributed something quite specific, except for Cordelia. So peeling her out of the cast of *Buffy* to join *Angel* was easily done. And changing her financial situation was an excellent tactic. Having made her somewhat nice, they could now make her even nicer as she learned to live as one of the monetarily challenged—or at least like an ordinary person.

It's all going to offer a lot of meat for Charisma as an actress, since she'll be able to find a whole new set of strengths and weaknesses in her character. She's always been one who's put in plenty of preparation, but has also left room for things to happen—going with her instinct, much like David. And, she says, after reading the script, "If I find something that I don't like, it's up to me to deliver it in a way that makes me happy and is true to [the character]." In other words, she's not a prima donna of any kind, not the type to throw a tantrum because Cordelia does something Charisma doesn't like. She's a professional, and works with the material she's given.

That, of course, has been true of all the cast members of *Buffy*. They've worked together to create a hit show. Now it's up to David and Charisma, as well as the others in the cast of *Angel*, to see whether the magic can be duplicated.

They'll have fun, and they'll have good material; that much is for sure. It remains solely in the hands of the viewers whether the show becomes a hit. Without any doubt, Charisma is excited at the prospect of the new show, even though it will mean even longer days for her as she takes on a larger role. That's fine, however; she's never been afraid of hard work, when it comes to something she loves. But she's been around the business long enough to understand that not all new shows—even those with impeccable pedigrees, spun off from successes—turn into winners. If it does well, her star will rise even higher. If not, then after a season she'll probably find herself looking for work again.

It's a gamble—but all acting is, as any actor knows. Sometimes the least likely thing can pay off, as David has shown. Even walking your dog can be an audition of sorts!

The inclusion of Cordelia in the cast of *Angel*, apart from providing some added links to, and continuity from, *Buffy the Vampire Slayer* also helps ensure a male audience for the show. There's little doubt that women love David and Angel. But he doesn't have a large following among men. Charisma, on the other hand, tall and beautiful, has plenty of male fans. Rather than bring in a new female lead, someone untried who might not go over well, it makes perfect sense to use a character who's been tried and tested. It not only strengthens the recognition factor in the cast, it offers—at least in theory—a built-in male audience, who'll gladly click their remotes to watch Charisma. As with every new show, it's a case of use every factor you can to give yourself an advantage over the competition. And Charisma is definitely a big advantage.

While she's thrilled by the new show, she's also understandably cautious. It doesn't come with any guarantee of success, so while she might be moving up in stature—from regular cast member to what amounts to female lead—and probably in salary, she's not about to splurge on a new house in the Hollywood Hills yet. Best to wait until the end of a successful first season for that kind of expense. And if she did move, it would be just her and her two retrievers—not too long ago she and her long-time boyfriend broke up.

While Sarah Michelle Gellar and Alyson Hannigan have both been active in movies, completing projects

(Alyson was most recently seen in *American Pie*, playing a character very different from Willow), many assume that Charisma has yet to make it to the big screen. That might seem odd, given her looks, and her acting ability, and, in fact, she has been involved in three films, all strictly independent features, and all largely unknown. There was *Josh Kirby—Time Warrior, Chapter 1—Planet of the Dino-Knights*, and its sequels, *Chapter 2—The Human Pets* and *Chapter 6— Last Battle for the Universe.* As to other, bigger roles, Charisma is in no big hurry.

"I'm ambitious, but I want balance," she explains. "And I'm not a tiger and I'm not a barracuda. I know what I have to do to excel, and that is I don't like to be running around to three, four appointments a day. I'm not going to get up and do something that I don't fell 100 percent about. I'm not going to get up and do something half-assed. And if I don't feel like I could get into it or love it, then I'm not going to do it."

Balance. It's a similar approach to David's, which would indicate that the two of them should work well together. They both prepare for their work, but are willing to give things a chance to go where they will. And, away from the set, they also share a mutual interest in the outdoors, although, in Charisma's case, that's more than just hiking an biking. She loves to climb, and not too long ago also discovered skydiving (she introduced Alyson Hannigan to the sport; reportedly, when the producers got wind of it, they asked the actresses to stop doing it for the length of their contracts, because of the danger).

If Cordelia can continue to grow—and there's no reason why she shouldn't—then she could well turn into the perfect foil for Angel. And although David and Charisma hadn't shared many scenes in the past, there's every indication that they'll do very well together onscreen, even if the romantic sparks probably won't fly between them. But not every male-female relationship has to be romantic, after all. It all bodes remarkably well for *Angel.*

CHAPTER TWELVE

DAVID

might play one of the most intense creatures on television, but in real life, he might just be one of the
most laid-back people in Los Angeles. Even when his
career seemed to be going nowhere, he didn't let any
stress about it get to him. He simply worked his jobs
to pay his rent and put food on the table, and kept on
trying. He had faith that it would all come right,
sooner or later. He believed in himself, and knew that
if he persevered, someone else would, too.

It's the kind of attitude that's all too rare. Most
people travel to L.A. wanting success and wanting it
now. David was a natural disciple of delayed gratifi-
cation. He believes, as he says, that "everything needs
to be right in order for it to work." And when he was
spotted while walking Bertha Blue, everything *was*
right. It was luck, it was pure Hollywood—but if he
hadn't had the talent to back up the luck, nothing
would have come of it. Fate had finally smiled on
him. He'd been in the right place at the right time,
with the right abilities.

He grew with *Buffy the Vampire Slayer*, much as
other members of the cast have. It was a show that
offered him the chance to develop his skills, and to

take chances that most shows wouldn't have given. After all, who would have thought that Angel could remain a heartthrob even after killing one of the recurring cast, and causing great mental anguish with his tricks to the heroine. But that's what happened. And by giving him another chance (after he'd duly paid for his sins), his character was rehabilitated.

Even more than the writers—who've done a remarkable job—it's David who's taken Angel to that next level, and made him worthy of his own series. Sarah Michelle Gellar has the male fans (and plenty of girls who admire the fact that she's a strong woman, the kind of character too often lacking as a role model on TV), but it's David who's won the women's hearts. That it could happen has been obvious from the moment he walked in for his first audition as Angel; but the way it's taken off from there has been nothing less than amazing.

For David, though, that's Angel, and not him. He spends a lot of time thinking about his character, but he recognizes that there's a huge gap between the man and the myth. Fame has come to him—he hasn't really pursued it, although it comes with the territory, and he's accepted that, somewhat reluctantly. He's at his happiest not being recognized, getting out for a round of golf, or a chance to hike or get on his mountain bike, to spend time with Ingrid, or just walk the dogs in peace and quiet.

Not that he doesn't appreciate his fans; he most definitely does. But fame hasn't gone—and never will go—to his head. He keeps a very human face on it all. He treats fans as people, not objects, given the lessons he learned from his father. He makes time for them, because he knows that without them, he doesn't have a job. Without them, there'd be no *Angel*.

Mostly, though, he makes time for a life. When he's not working, he's not running after other projects or trying to make himself into a greater celebrity by being seen in all the right clubs, all the right places. He doesn't need that. At the core, David is comfortable with himself and his place in the world. He has a strong sense of who he is, and he likes himself. He can relax, read a book, play with the dogs, enjoy free time with Ingrid. It's an enviable position, and one that most actors never seem to achieve.

The night time colors that make up Angel's wardrobe might look good on David's body, but they're not really him. He doesn't need blacks, or purple velvets to make him who is he is. Instead of the brooding, there's an openness about him, a warmth. He doesn't need to keep a distance. About the only thing he really craves more of are those Philly cheesesteak sandwiches (like any local dish, the ones in Los Angeles just aren't the same!).

It's a good life he's carved out for himself. He works hard—during the season his hours are very long and draining—but he does get free time. And, in all likelihood, this will pave the way to his real dream, which is to direct, to fashion a career on the other side of the camera. Other actors have done it (Ron Howard immediately springs to mind) with a great deal of success, and David's grounding at Ithaca, where he got his degree in film, has certainly prepared him for it.

But for a career that really began by accident, acting has proved to be a good path for him. The love of it has always been there, but never the realization that it could be him up there. Once that arrived, it was natural talent (okay, and looks) that helped him become successful—after a while.

David Boreanaz is proof that, with persistence and faith in yourself, you really can achieve your goals. He's also proof that life isn't always a straight line, and that meandering down the back roads can be quite rewarding in the long run. You make the most of what life hands you, both the good and the band—it all evens out in the end.

While Angel might brood, that's a quality you won't really find in David. He might meditate on things and ideas, but his low-key, outgoing nature is more likely to wear a smile than a tortured grimace. So the fact that he's well known, and well loved, for his brooding is actually a testament to his acting skills.

He's worked hard to find the points where David can intersect with Angel, and where he can truly enter the character. As the role has expanded, and more back story has been provided, in some ways it's become easier. But it's also been harder, since Angel is now more defined. The audience knows more about him, and what makes him tick. As the intensity level on the show was raised for Angel, so David's job became more of a challenge. But that's exactly what he's always sought in acting—something to keep him pushing, and keep him working.

For someone with no formal acting background, he's proved to be naturally adept in the craft. Reading a lot has helped, and so did trying things on stage. But his true growth has come with *Buffy*, and with *Angel* he will truly soar.

And then what? People are already eager to cast him in movie roles, although David remains reluctant to jump on that particular bandwagon. In all likelihood, he will at some point—possibly next summer—if the right script becomes available. But it would never simply be for the sake of getting his name on the big screen. He keeps a tough quality control around.

David obviously loves acting—he wouldn't have spent so long doing low-rent jobs otherwise, while waiting for things to happen. And that means he'll be acting for a long time. But he's educated and curious, and the crossover to working on the other side of the camera might hold more artistic satisfaction for him in the long run. Not immediately, obviously (although if *Angel* is the runaway success everyone hopes it will be, then maybe he'll get to direct an episode or two), but somewhere down the line, it might well be David's name appearing in the direction credits.

It's doubtful that he'd take on any other roles involving vampires or anything supernatural. He's already had the best, and while they'll certainly be offered to him, he's been there and done that, and has no wish to be typecast, thank you very much. The whole point of acting is to keep pushing at himself, not repeat the same thing over and over.

At the moment, the whole world is a plum for David, ripe and ready to be eaten. Rather than gulp it all down, he's happy to savor it in small, slow bites, and enjoy each one in his mouth. That way you enjoy it much more.

He's a happy man, in every aspect of his life. Being married to Ingrid fulfills him; he's found the ideal woman to be his life partner. In another ten years there'll likely be another Boreanaz or two running around and growing up. Keeping that part of his life sheltered from the public eye is deliberate—there are some areas to which strangers shouldn't be allowed access.

It's amazing how one thing can completely change a life. For David, *Buffy the Vampire Slayer* has altered everything. It's turned him from a nobody (at least as an actor—he was always *somebody*) into a star, given him his own show, fans, more money than he could have imagined back when he was struggling. The show has been very good to him. But if it hadn't been that, then it would have been something else, somewhere, sometime. He had the faith to believe that, and it's probably true.

The when and how is all somehow academic now; he's arrived in the hearts and minds of a lot of people, and very soon there will be a lot more who'll succumb to the charms of Angel. By letting it build gradually, David has allowed things to come naturally—and he's more comfortable with that than with anything forced.

To be sure, there's a lot of the hippie in David (and more than just his love of the Grateful Dead!), all lightly tinged with some New Age ideas. He's not exactly your average vampire icon. But that's part of the attraction, both of the man and of his character.

He's doing something he loves, and it shows in his performances. He relishes every scene he has, and plays it the best way he can. No coasting. And he loves his life. And he never forgets that without Bertha Blue, things might not have reached their time. He no longer needs the job to keep his dogs in food— even the best gourmet dog food—but he's never likely to forget what it was like at the bottom.

David Boreanaz is a man of many facets, as complex as the Southern California days are long. He won't be easily unraveled and explained. But a little mystery remains a good thing—that way there are more secrets to slowly be revealed and treasured.

Angel is real, at least when David assumes the character. And *Angel* looks to have a long life. Maybe not another two hundred and forty some years, but still plenty. It's all come together so perfectly that it can't be anything other than fate. And that would suit David perfectly. It's karma.

He's perfectly poised between the past and future, standing very firmly on the present. To say his time is now would be correct, but it would also be something of an understatement. *Angel* will almost certainly be a success, but it won't last forever; every show has its own shelf life. However, it does open up plenty of possibilities for the future. On the stage, David has played outsiders, schizophrenics, people debilitated by age, and it's those outsiders who interest him—much as *Angel* is one of the ultimate outsiders. In future film roles, for example, he'd love to play in a Western, portraying a cowboy, although, when he was younger, he always found himself rooting for the Indians. But cowboys were outsiders, away from the civilized mainstream of society. Their lives, in actuality, didn't revolve around gunplay and the destruction of the Native American culture, although that's the way they were often portrayed in the past. And, of course, should the chance ever occur, David wouldn't turn down a role in one of the upcoming *Star Wars* films! And who could blame him—in the past the movies have sent several careers into the stratosphere.

Acting has become as much a part of him as breathing. The love of it that was fostered in him when he was young has, completely unexpectedly, grown into a career. But that's the way life sometimes goes.

As to directing, well, that will wait. There's a great deal to explore in front of the camera first, and so far that's only really been the tip of the iceberg. *Angel* promises to offer David the opportunity to explore many other facets of his character, to make Angel more adult, and to deal with an entirely different set of problems to the ones he faced on *Buffy*. In all likelihood, the reversion to a completely evil state won't be among them, but with Joss Whedon at the helm, you should never say never; he's proved himself to be a master at guiding shows through unlikely turns and making them work.

With a very stable home life (which he prefers to keep personal—in one online chat, he refused to say whether or not he was even married), and a good balance between work and pleasure, David is able to throw himself wholeheartedly into his acting. He has one of the plum roles on television, certainly one of the deepest and most complicated, an ideal character for the times in which we live, with the Millennium fast approaching.

From the very first moment he walked in to audition as Angel, there's been no doubt that he was perfectly suited to the role. The fit was so right that it could almost have been written expressly for him. And without a doubt, he's completely made it his own—it would be impossible to imagine anyone else ever playing Angel. And that is the beauty of it all, some absolutely ideal casting.

Wherever Angel does go on his new show—and some of the territory will probably be psychological—

he will push at the boundaries, just as he has in the past. David will have a great deal of meat in his scripts, a chance to tackle a wide range of issues, both within and outside himself. The others will help, of course, but the attention will probably remain quite firmly centered on him (although, like *Buffy*, there will probably be episodes that really focus on the other characters and their lives and dilemmas).

Eventually a career on the other side of the camera will beckon to David. After all, he did study film for four years. But that change won't happen anytime soon. And when it does, it will probably happen in the same way David has undertaken everything so far—when the time is right, it will come to him.

In the meantime there's a great deal to be enjoyed, by David, and by everyone who watches him. He's proved that angels don't all have to fly. Some can soar without ever leaving the ground.

1971 May 16	David Boreanaz born in Buffalo, NY, to David Roberts and his wife, Patti. The family moves to Philadelphia, where Roberts becomes a TV weatherman, and David attends the exclusive, private Malvern Prep School.
1987	David graduates from Malvern Prep a year early. He'd played on the football team until sidelined by a knee injury, and had frequently attended theatrical performances in New York. From Philadelphia, he moves to Ithaca, NY, to attend Ithaca College, where he studies film.
1991	David graduates from Ithaca College with a degree in film and moves west to Los Angeles, center of the film industry.
1992	Employed as a prop master, David is hired to act in his first commercial, for Foster's beer. It never airs. Bitten by the acting bug, David tries to pursue an acting career. Initially all he manages are a couple of uncredited roles in movies— *Aspen Extreme* and *Best of the Best II*.
1993	David wins a role in the movie *Eyes of the World*, which is never released, then

lands his first television role, playing the biker boyfriend of Kelly on the "Movie Show" episode of *Married . . . with Children* on the Fox Network.

1994   David appears in his first stage role, in the play *Hatful of Rain*.

1995   He is in another stage play, *Italian-American Reconciliation*. To earn money, for the last several years he's held a series a jobs, anything from parking cars to selling frozen meat to a truck to emptying portable toilets to handing out towels at a health club.

1996   David performs in an Equity waiver production of *Fool for Love*. A little while later, while walking Bertha Blue, he's "discovered" by a manager. The next day, thanks to the manager, he reads for the part of Angel in a new series due to air the fall on the upstart WB Network— *Buffy the Vampire Slayer*. David wins the role. During the first season he meets, and begins dating an Irish social worker living in Los Angeles, Ingrid.

1997   The first season of Buffy proves successful, and the show is renewed, with David's role much expanded in the second season. Angel and Buffy make love, Angel reverts to his vampire status, and at the end of the season Buffy has no choice but to dispatch him to hell. The character of Angel has become so popular, however, that after the season finale has aired, it is announced that Angel will be getting his own spin-off series in the 1999–2000 season.

1998   During the break following the second season, David takes a vacation trip to Africa. After he returns, he and Ingrid marry. The third season of *Buffy* begins, and Angel returns from hell. David also becomes a spokesman for Levi's Original Spin program, making promotional appearances around the country, designing some custom jeans that are auctioned off to help the organization Peace 2000.

1999   The delayed season finale of *Buffy* airs.
July 13   It had been held back for seven weeks following the tragic shooting in Littleton, Colorado. Immediately after the show, the first promotional clip for *Angel* is shown.

September   *Angel* debuts on the WB, immediately following *Buffy* on the schedule.

DAVID BOREANAZ—PROFESSIONAL

APPEARANCES

FILM

Aspen Extreme (1993)
Paul Gross, Peter Berg, Finola Hughes, Teri Polo, Martin Kemp, Nicoletta Scorsese. Directed and written by Patrick Hasburgh. David's appearance is uncredited.

Best of the Best II (1993)
Eric Roberts, Philip Rhee, Christopher Penn, Ralph Moeller, Wayne Newton, Meg Foster, Edan Gross. Directed by Robert Radler. Written by John Allen Nelson and Max Strom. David's appearance is uncredited.

Eyes of the World (1993)
Unreleased.

STAGE PLAYS

Hatful of Rain (1994)
Italian-American Reconciliation (1995)
Fool for Love (1996)*
*Note: This was an Equity waiver production, meaning that the theater contained 99 seats or less, allowing the play to be performed without members of Equity, the actors' union.

TELEVISION

Married. . . . with Children (1993)
"The Movie Show." David's plays Frank, the biker

boyfriend of Kelly Bundy (Christina Applegate).
Buffy the Vampire Slayer (1996–1999)
David plays Angel.
Angel (1999—)
David appears in the title role.

DAVID BOREANAZ—THE QUICK FACTS

Born: May 16, 1971, Buffalo, NY.

Star sign: Taurus.

Height: 6' 1".

Hand preference: Right-handed.

High school: Malvern Prep, Philadelphia, PA.

College: Ithaca College, Ithaca, NY.

Current residence: Los Angeles, CA.

Marital status: Married to Ingrid, an Irish social worker.

Children: None.

Pets: Two dogs, Bertha Blue, a mixed breed, and a Chinese Crested.

Hobbies: Hiking, mountain biking, reading, music.

Favorite band: Grateful Dead.

Favorite author: Og Mandino.

Favorite book: *Joe Louis: The Great Black Hope* by Richard Bak.

Favorite actors: Gary Oldman, Al Pacino.

Favorite actress: Gwyneth Paltrow.

Favorite comic book: *Spiderman*.

Favorite foods: Eggs benedict, Philly cheesesteak
    sandwiches.

Favorite sports: Golf, basketball, football.

Automobiles: Black Mercedes sedan, black 1996 Ford
    Explorer.

GET THE 411 ON YOUR FAVORITE
SINGERS!

B*WITCHED
0-312-97360-8___$4.99___$6.50 Can.

BACKSTREET BOYS
0-312-96853-1___$3.99___$4.99 Can.

BRANDY
0-312-97055-2___$4.99___$6.50 Can.

FIVE
0-312-97225-3___$4.99___$6.50 Can.

LAURYN HILL
0-312-97210-5___$5.99___$7.99 Can.

RICKY MARTIN
0-312-97322-5___$4.99___$6.50 Can.

THE MOFFATTS
0-312-97359-4___$4.99___$6.50 Can.

98°
0-312-97200-8___$4.99___$6.50 Can.

N SYNC
0-312-97198-2___$4.99___$6.50 Can.

BRITNEY SPEARS
0-312-97268-7___$4.99___$6.50 Can.